PEACOCKS ONLY

A Survival Guide for Peacocks

VOL. III

DEDICATION

It is difficult to write a dedication page for this work on the keeping and care of peacocks because it has been a group effort. But with that being said, a large slice of the credit must be served up to Becky Dembowski. Without her enthusiasm and skill, this information for peacock lovers everywhere would have never gotten into print.

Linda Smith Potts must also be mentioned for her work as a Moderator to our Facebook group of 24,000 members that can be found as: Peacocks Only. Linda has shared her expertise in genetics and practical skills with our group from its beginning in 2014. She continues to be one of the mainstays of the group.

Craig Hopkins is another valuable resource for Peacock care. We are grateful to him for contributing his articles to this book. He has committed a lifetime to the breeding and health of Peacocks. But more than that, he has generously given his time to educate others on their care.

Our group expert, Lenore Price, has contributed tirelessly to address the concerns of the Peacocks Only group members. She is a primary strength of the group. We have all benefited greatly from her service.

Let us not forget the Peacocks Only group members who are so friendly and helpful to all that have inquiries and concerns about the health, hatching, feeding, and care of their peacocks. They are the true strength of the group.

All Rights Reserved

No part of this book may be used or reproduced by any means,

Graphic, electronic, or mechanical, including photocopying,

Recording or taping or by an information storage retrieval system

Without the written permission of the author,

Except in the case of brief quotations

Embodied in critical articles and reviews.

ISBN: 9798863994000

Illustrations © 2023 Alicia Pezzente

Cover photographs were taken by Douglas Buffington

2024 Vol. 3

You can learn more and interact with other peacock enthusiasts through our Facebook group "Peacocks Only".

Copyright ©2020 by Douglas Buffington

DISCLAIMER

This book is not intended as a substitute for the medical advice of a veterinarian. The reader should regularly consult a veterinarian in matters relating to his/her birds' health and particularly with respect to any symptoms that may require diagnosis or medical attention. The information in this book is meant to supplement, not replace, proper veterinarian care and diagnosis.

PEACOCKS ONLY

A SURVIVAL GUIDE FOR PEACOCKS

Author: Douglas Buffington

Cover Illustrator: Alicia Pezzente

TABLE OF CONTENTS

1. Pre & Postseason Regimen……………………..……8

2. Diseases Transmitted to Eggs……………………….8

3. How to Incubate Peacock Eggs…………................11

4. Incubator Temperatures…………………………….13

5. Incubator Placement………………………………. 15

6. Keep the Heat Lamp On…………………………...15

7. Keeping Chicks Healthy…………………………...16

8. All Starter Feeds Are Not Created Equal………….19

9. Buying Fertile Peacock Eggs………………………21

10. Diseases of Peafowl……………………………...23

11. Doug's Bits and Pieces…………………………...32

12. Intramuscular Medication Dosing of Peafowl…….35

13. Heated Roost for Peafowl………………………...38

14. Swelling of the Eye Sinuses……………………...40

15. Gaping Bird Diagnosis and Treatment…………...42

16. Moxivet Plus……………………………………..45

17. How to Treat a Sick Peacock…………………….46

18. Blackhead Treatment……………………………………..49

19. Transporting Peacocks……………………………....…51

20. Can you Raise Chickens, Turkeys and Peafowl Together..51

21. Three Things that kill a Peacock, Pheasant & Turkeys…..53

22. Poultry Species as Blackhead Reservoir……………..….58

23. Blackhead Transmission by Cecal Worm Eggs & Soil…..59

24. Calcium: The Key to Beautiful Eggs and Healthy Hen…..60

25. Fowl Pox…………………………………………….....61

26. Internal Parasites of Peacocks, Pheasants & Turkey……..62

27. Medicated Starter…..…………………………….....…..66

28. Oral Medication Dosing of Peafowl…….......……………67

29. Protozoan Diseases Common to Peafowl……………..…..69

30. Permethrin 10% premises spray………………………….71

31. Protozoans that can kill Peacocks, Pheasants & Turkeys...72

32. Wormer Medications……..………………………….....75

33. No Chicks in the Bathtub Please………………....……..78

34. Blackhead, Coccidiosis, Canker Treatment……………….80

35. All in One Powder………….…………………….….…..82

36. The Truth About Feeding Peacocks, Pheasants &Turkey...83

37. Everything You Need to Know About Wry Neck………..84

38. What You Need to Know about MG & MS……………...87

39. What is Aspergillosis and How to Prevent it…………....90

40. General care of Peacocks………………………….…..93

41. Nesting Boxes for Peafowl…………………………...98

42. Flight Pen Construction…………….…………..........99

43. Pavo Muticus (Green) Peafowl……………………...…103

44. Blending Feeds is Not a Good Idea……………….........105

45. Egg Binding……………………………………...…...106

46. Are Pumpkin Seeds a Dewormer……………….….….108

47. Peacock Medications in the UK & EU……………….110

48. What to Feed a Peacock……………….……………..111

49. Syringing Medications…………………………….…113

50. What to Remember About Blackhead and Canker….…...114

51. How Amprolium Works……………………………..…,…115

52. Gapeworms………………………………..…………116

52. What Canker Looks Like……………………………...118

53. Medications to Keep on Hand……………………….119

54. Trichomoniasis (Canker)……………………….……120

55. Canker Treatment (Trichomoniasis)…..………….……121

56. Do not bring Peacocks home from the auction……………125

PEACOCKS

Peacocks are the most royal, regal, and beautiful of all birds that could grace a farm, ranch, estate, or country home. Like all things of beauty, they come to us with their own requirements of tender care. At the same time, peacocks are not like growing orchids but they are a little more than zinnias. Now that you have them home with you, what is next?

There are peacock pens, peacock shelters, feed, and medications to prepare. Then there will be peacock egg incubation, hatching, and chick-rearing. For the beginner, all of this will seem like an endless maze. On the pages, you will find the map that will take you from incubating an egg to the full beauty of a grown peacock. We know you will enjoy the journey and be hooked for life.

THE FOLLOWING IS EVERYTHING DOUG KNOWS ABOUT PEACOCKS

I am not a Veterinarian and I do not accept responsibility for how the information presented here is used. **This book is a compilation of articles that are presented in no particular order.** They are contributed by Doug Buffington, Craig Hopkins, the Freedom Ranger Hatchery, Veterinarians, University Professors and others.

PRE & POST SEASON REGIMEN

by: Doug Buffington

The objective of a preseason, preventative regimen is to clean the birds up before the first eggs are laid. It can be given again after the laying season is over to get your Peacocks ready for winter. During March, it is a good practice to give your flock a 5 to 7 day treatment of the All in One which has the Levamisole wormer as one of its ingredients. All in One is a pigeon medication that can be therapeutic for any bird from a Canary to an Ostrich. It has ingredients to treat a flock for Coccidiosis, Canker, Hexamita, and Blackhead protozoans as well as worms. Ten days after the All-in-One treatment is completed, it should be followed by one round of another recommended worm medication. The second worming will kill the worms that have hatched from the worm eggs left by the worms that were expelled by the All-in-One treatment. Follow this practice and your flock will go into the laying season in the best possible health which will translate into a better egg production and a better hatch rate. Repeat this regimen in the early fall to get your peacocks ready for the Winter. The All in One can be found at Pigeon Supplies Plus and other pigeon supply sites. Double the dose when treating acutely sick birds drinking normally.

Diseases Transmitted to Eggs

By: Margaret A. Wissman, D.V.M., D.A.B.V.P.

Early embryonic death, blood ring, dead-in-shell......these terms frustrate and confound aviculturists, novice and professional alike. The reasons that embryos die are many, and diagnosing the specific cause of death can prove elusive in many cases. A serious aviculturist, whether a hobbyist or one who makes a living from breeding birds, should seek to work with an experienced avian veterinarian who can help with all facets of aviculture. Every egg embryo that dies prior to hatching should be examined by an avian veterinarian who can perform an egg necropsy and any other tests that may help to determine the cause of death. Often, histopathology (microscopic examination of tissues) will prove diagnostic, if the embryo has recently died. Bacterial and fungal cultures, stains of egg membranes, viral isolation and DNA PCR probes for specific organisms may help in diagnosing the cause of death.

There are many infectious organisms that can be transferred from the hen to the egg that may cause the egg to die. In some cases, the infectious organism may infect the egg, yet the embryo may continue developing, and may even hatch, carrying the organism at hatch time. If an organism is passed from an infected hen directly into an egg and then into the developing embryo, this is called **vertical transmission.** The term vertical transmission is also used to describe the transmission of an infectious agent from a parent to an egg during fertilization, during egg development in the oviduct of the hen, or immediately after oviposition. Once the egg is laid, some infectious organisms can pass through the eggshell upon contact with contaminated feces, urates, or bedding. This is also considered vertical transmission if infection occurs immediately after laying. Some organisms are transmitted from the ovary to the egg, and this is called *transovarian transmission*. Infectious organisms harbored in the oviduct can also be passed into the egg prior to the shell being formed. Some organisms can infect eggs if contents from the cloaca contaminate the surface of the eggs, and then penetrate the egg. The other method of transmission of infectious organisms is by *horizontal transmission*. Some ways that horizontal transmission occurs are by preening, inhalation, copulation, insect or animal bites, ingestion, contact with contaminated equipment or fighting.

It seems obvious that prior to the egg membranes and shell being applied to it, the egg would be susceptible to infection by numerous infectious organisms. Even though the eggshell appears solid, it contains microscopic pores that can allow liquids and organisms of small enough size into the egg. The pores allow the transfer of gasses, as well.

Bacterial Diseases

Chlamydia psittaci is a primitive bacteria that can be vertically transmitted from an infected hen through the egg to the embryo. Depending on the pathogenicity of the strain and the number of organisms that are passed into the egg, the embryo may die during incubation, or it may actually hatch as a baby bird with chlamydiosis. It should be noted that transovarian transmission of chlamydiosis has not yet been confirmed by researchers, so it may be that the eggs are contaminated with the organism by some other vertical method.

Bacteria of the genus *Salmonella* can also cause embryos to die in the shell, or if the egg is contaminated by a very small number of bacteria, *Salmonella* can cause weak hatch babies that may die shortly after breaking out of the egg. The bacteria may cause yolk material to coagulate in the egg, and dead embryos may show hemorrhagic streaks on the liver. The spleen and kidneys may be congested. Pinpoint areas of the liver may be necrotic. Inflammation of the pericardium may also be seen. *Salmonella* are isile bacteria that can penetrate the eggshell and can be transmitted vertically. The culture of the infected embryo will prove diagnostic.

Some *Staphylococcus* bacteria can kill embryos. The avian embryo can be resistant to some strains of staphylococci but can be highly susceptible to other strains. Infected wounds on parent birds can infect eggs, as can staph infections found on the hands of aviculturists if the egg comes in contact with lesions. Artificial incubators will grow staph readily, and it can spread horizontally in this manner. An embryo can die within 48 hours of exposure to some strains of staph, especially *Staph. aureus*. The older the embryo is at the time of first exposure to staph, the less chance of embryonic mortality. Hemorrhages may be found on various internal organs. A laying hen can develop an ovary infected with *Staph. faecalis*, which can contaminate the forming egg. Contaminated eggs will have up to 50% mortality.

E. coli is a common bacterium normally found in the GI tract of mammals, and some birds, as well. It can enter the egg from an infected reproductive tract of a hen. *E. coli* can also penetrate through the eggshell if the egg is contaminated with fecal material. *E. coli* commonly causes yolk sac infection, causing the yolk sac contents to appear watery and yellow-green or yellow-brown. Dirty nests can serve as sources of contamination to eggs. The use of water bottles can reduce the amount of *E. coli* that builds up in the GI tract of birds. Farms that use a watering system and not water bowls seem to have fewer problems with sub-clinical bacterial infections in their breeder birds and their offspring. Many embryos infected with *E. coli* will die late in incubation or shortly after hatching.

If an *E. coli* infection is acquired during incubation, the hatchling may develop an umbilical and yolk sac infection (omphalitis) and they may have poor weight gain. Cracked eggs are more easily infected and may serve as a source of infection for other eggs in the incubator. Cracked eggs should be repaired as soon as the damage is discovered, or they should be discarded.

Mycoplasma

Mycoplamatales are one order of microscopic organisms that replicate by binary fission. They have no cell wall, but have a three-layer membrane. They are more primitive than bacteria, and must live and grow inside the host. In the environment they live only for a short time. Although we have much to learn about *mycoplasmas*, they can be involved in problems, conjunctivitis and respiratory infections, and also respiratory/eye problems in other species of pet and breeder birds. The organism is spread by the respiratory excretions and by the gonads of both sexes, and infection in the air sacs can lead to contact transmission of the ovary and developing follicle. Transovarian transmission can occur. *Mycoplasma* can spread to the egg from an infected oviduct or from the semen of infected male birds.

It is possible to treat eggs infected with *Mycoplasma* infections. Tylosin is injected into the air cell at the start of incubation. A combination of lincomycin and spectinomycin is also effective for egg injection. Dipping the eggs in antibiotic solutions is effective in reducing the incidence of disease.

HOW TO INCUBATE PEACOCK EGGS

by: Doug Buffington

Chicken eggs will tolerate swings in the incubator temperature and humidity levels and still hatch well enough. Peacock eggs will require more precise settings. People do not get too alarmed if the chicken hatch rate is lower than expected. After all, more eggs are coming tomorrow. However, the eggs of peafowl have a limited season. Good hatch rates with peacock eggs will require a good grip on the temperature and humidity. Even then, peacock eggs will not hatch at the same rate as chicken eggs.

Most know the recommended hatching temperature is **99.5** degrees. But few understand how to measure and set the correct humidity at **60%**. First, the incubator must be placed in a room where the ambient humidity is stable. Open sheds, barns, and shops will not achieve this objective. Next, the humidity inside the incubator must be set at **60%**...especially if the incubating and hatching is taking place in the same cabinet. This will result in a Wet Bulb reading between **86** and **88** degrees.

If you have a separate hatcher, the humidity should be **70%** during the last three days of the hatch. If you incubate and hatch in the same cabinet, you should be able to achieve **70%** by standing one or two GQF wicks in the water tray. Place it a long ways to the fan if the water tray will allow it. There is only one way to correctly measure humidity. It is to take an old fashion "wet bulb" reading. If you are hatching and at the same time incubating other eggs in the same cabinet, at the same time, a humidity of **60%** is recommended. The water tray in a GQF incubator can be replaced with a large 9x15", low profile type of Tupper Ware-like container.

Adjusting the humidity will require that the ventilation of the incubator be increased or decreased. More ventilation will lower the humidity and less will increase it. On a cabinet incubator, fully open the intake vent and vary the exhaust vents to achieve the desired humidity. Adjusting the humidity is not a quick process. The readings will need to be observed over a couple of days. A wet-bulb reading of **86** to **88** (30c) will put you in the range of **60%** humidity. Once the humidity is set and the incubator is not moved, the humidity will remain fixed.

If an incubator cabinet will allow it, lay the eggs on their side. Use jumbo egg trays turned upside down for incubating on the side. Turn the eggs 180 degrees twice daily in addition to the automatic turning. If eggs must be incubated pointed end down, be sure to rotate the eggs 1/4 turn each twice day in addition to the automatic turning.

Do not depend on the digital instruments from Walmart to provide an accurate measure of humidity or temperature. Also, don't depend on the digital incubator readouts from the incubator. Find a reliable thermometer to check the temperature and use a wet bulb reading to set the humidity. This is the only way to know what is going on inside the incubator.

INCUBATOR TEMPERATURES

by: Doug Buffington

It is hard to get a straight answer for an acceptable temperature to incubate eggs. Even the makers of the GQF incubators will not tell you. But their incubators come set on 100 degrees. However, a number of universities that teach agricultural science will recommend a temperature between **99** and **100** degrees as optimal. Caution should be exercised when temperatures begin to fluctuate between **98** and **102**. An incubator constantly running even a degree below **99** will not kill the embryo but many of your chicks will hatch with "toe curl." Temperatures of **103** and higher will kill your egg embryos.

Incubator settings of **99.5**f (37.5c) are most often recommended because this setting will allow a temporary variance of one degree in either direction without harming the eggs. Temporary spikes and dips that can be quickly corrected will not likely harm the eggs. But eggs may temporarily drop to as low as 80 during a power outage. So, those who experience a temporary power outage will need to wrap the incubator with a blanket and hope the power is restored soon. Consider acquiring a generator for these emergencies.

Craig Hopkins, at hopkinslivestock.com, hatches hundreds of peacock eggs each year. He recommends running both the hatcher and incubator at a temperature of **99.5** with a humidity of **60%** in the incubator and **70%** for the hatcher. However, if eggs are being hatched while other eggs are being incubated at the same time in the same incubator, the humidity can remain at 60%. For those running a separate hatcher, using the same temperature and humidity settings as the incubator will allow an overflow of eggs to be placed in the hatcher. But a dedicated hatcher, used only as such, should maintain a humidity of **70%**. All the above information is for an incubator with a fan or what is called a "forced air" incubator. Incubators without a fan are "still air" incubators and should be running at 101 degrees or as the manufacturer recommends. The explanation is that a higher temperature is necessary to properly warm the bottom of the eggs in the absence of a fan to circulate the heat. The water pan in still-air incubators should be filled twice daily.

For those who are experiencing the difficulty of finding a reliable thermometer, you should select a thermometer from the store rack that agrees with the majority of the others. Hang the thermometer with the bulb midway in the incubator. The best reading of the day will be from the window in the door during the morning before the incubator or hatcher is opened for the first time.

The temperature readings need to be taken with the door closed. Many cabinet incubators will come with a window in them. Those who do not have a window should cut a window in the door and install a piece of Plexiglas over it. The window should allow a view of all three trays. It can be a narrow window that measures, 6 inches wide and 24 inches tall. The thermometer should be hung midway in the incubator. A window will also allow a view of the hatch without opening the door.

About the Humidity……A wet bulb reading is the only way to accurately measure the incubator humidity. It should read between **86** and **88** degrees to maintain a humidity of **60%** which is good for both incubating and hatching the eggs of peafowl in the absence of a dedicated hatcher. The desired level of humidity will be achieved by adjusting the ventilation on your incubator. If your humidity is set on **60%** it can easily be raised to **70%** during hatching by standing one or two GQF wicks in the water tray. If you are hatching while other eggs are incubating in the same incubator at the same time, you can leave your humidity set at **60%**. The water tray in a GQF incubator can be replaced with a large 9x15", low profile type of Tupper Ware like container.

Remember, you simply cannot depend on the digital thermometers and humidity gauges from Walmart or from anywhere else.

Be sure to incubate peacock eggs by laying them on their side with the pointed end slightly down. In addition to the automatic rotation, turn the eggs 180 degrees twice daily to improve the hatch rate. Jumbo plastic egg trays turned upside down will serve well for this purpose.

Doug's Note: If eggs must be placed pointed end down, be sure to rotate the egg **1/4** turn twice daily in addition to the automatic turning.

INCUBATOR PLACEMENT
by: Doug Buffington

In order for incubators to maintain a fixed level of temperature and humidity, they must be placed in an environment where the ambient levels are stable. Shops, open sheds and back porches are poor choices to locate an incubator.

When the ambient level of humidity fluctuates it will cause the humidity level in the incubator to likewise fluctuate. Fluctuating temperatures will also affect the incubator function. If the ambient temperature is too low, the incubator will not be able to maintain its setting. When the ambient temperature approaches 90 degrees the incubator will cease to function properly. I wish I had a more technical explanation for you but your eggs will not hatch properly in an overheated room. And, of course, there should be no toxic fumes to pull in and blow over your eggs.

KEEP THE HEAT LAMP ON
by: Doug Buffington

Each year, some breeders will present sick chicks that are dying. When ask about the heat lamp they relate that due to hot daytime temperatures, they have been turning it off during the day. Some have also turned it off during the night too. Lastly, there are those who have their chicks inside under the air conditioning with no heat lamp. A young chick will not have the body mass or the feathers to hold body heat. And, more than any other chick, peachicks seem to crave heat. Even the older chicks in a grow-out pen will group under a lamp at night.

If your coop is large enough for the chicks to escape the heat of the lamp when they feel too warm they will be fine...especially if they are not panting. Lay a thermometer flat under the lamp. It should not read more than 95 degrees. Build your coops to a spacious 8x3x3 on legs. They will need to stay in it for their first 4 months while their immune systems develop resistance to Coccidiosis and Blackhead.

As the summer grinds, on you can adjust the heat by raising the lamp or by changing to a lower wattage bulb. In warmer climates, try to avoid using the 250 watt red lamps like the those at McDonalds to keep the hamburgers hot. An 80 to 90 watt flood lamp may be adequate for cooler, ambient temperatures with as little as 25 to 40 watts for warmer weather. Government regulations are replacing incandescent lighting with LED bulbs that will not produce heat. However, incandescent heat lamps and appliance bulbs will still be available.

Here is the take away.

1. Keep the chicks off the ground for the first 4 months.
2. Be liberal with your coop size like 8x3x3 on legs.
3. Maintain a temperature of not more than 90 to 95 degrees directly under the lamp. Check by laying a thermometer flat under the lamp.
4. Adjust the bulb wattage if needed as the summer progresses. Or, you can raise or lower the lamp. Provide space for the chicks to escape the heat to find their comfort zone.

KEEPING CHICKS HEALTHY

by: Doug Buffington

Ruling out poor management, there are only three things that most commonly kill chicks as well as grown peacocks. They are bacterial infections, protozoan infections (blackhead and coccidiosis) and worms.

When they are on the ground, chicks will begin to pick up bacterial infections, protozoans and worms. It is recommended that chicks be cooped up on wire, off the ground, for their first 3 to 4 months. It takes that long for a peacock's immune system to acquire its resistance to the Coccidiosis and Blackhead protozoans.

Good chick health begins with the All in One medication flock treatment before the laying season. Salmonella, Ecoli, Mycoplasma and a large number of other bacterial diseases can be vertically transmitted to an egg. Deworming a flock will reduce the Blackhead protozoan load transmitted by the Cecal worm as well as evacuate other worms that damage the hen's intestines. The All in One has an antibiotic, a dewormer and the antiprotozoal ingredients to combat Coccidiosis and Blackhead. It also has amino acids, electrolytes, vitamins and probiotics as ingredients. The All in One will not only reduce the protozoan burden that hens carry but also help eliminate any subclinical bacterial infections that may be vertically transmitted to the eggs and embryos. Elevated protozoan levels will kill Peafowl, Turkey and Pheasants. Heavy worm populations will do the same. Remember, Cecal worms will carry the Blackhead protozoan.

Bacteria transferred from the hen to the egg can kill the embryo. If an infected chick survives, it will die shortly after the hatch but not before transmitting bacterial disease to other chicks. This is one cause of "coop death." This is a term used to describe those chicks that die in the coop from undetermined causes. If you find chicks dying in the coop at any age, it is recommended to medicate all of those in the same coop with the All in One. Use a quarter teaspoon per pint of water or 2 tsp per gallon.

Good chick health will also require a coop to be pressure washed or otherwise well cleaned especially if a chicken has ever been in it. Chickens are resistant carriers of worms, Coccidios and Blackhead. It is recommended that a good cleaning be followed with a Tec Trol disinfectant spray. Tec Trol is a little expensive but one gallon will last a lifetime because the usage only requires 1/2 ounce per gallon of water. This works out to be a capful. Those at the 800 phone line for Tec Trol say that there is no shelf life to the product and that it is good even after 20 years. The best prices for Tec Trol can be found on Ebay. Be sure to consider the shipping cost when comparing prices.

Despite the number of warnings on the label, Tec Trol is pleasant to smell and it does not seem harmful in dilution although you should never get any chemical into your eyes. Also, Tec Trol is not corrosive to metal. But attention should be given to the label when determining those surfaces to be avoided. You can spray coops, walls, floors and incubators with Tec Trol. It is the very best disinfectant for farm use. Again, as with all chemicals, you should avoid getting it into your eyes.

Tec Trol also advertises its product as a disinfectant for eggs. Dirty eggs can be easily cleaned. Mix up a spray bottle of Tec Trol solution. Crumple up a couple of paper towels. Spray the towels until damp. Gently press the egg into the crumple and rotate it. The dirt and whatever else will easily come off. Be sure to wash your hands both before and after sanitizing eggs. However, many are only cleaning the dirtiest eggs. Others may be wiped with a dry paper towel. The complaint is often made that wet washing eggs will remove the layer of protein, covering the egg, that most like to keep intact. The belief is that removing the protein layer will lower the hatch rate. This covering is often called the "bloom."

Now, back to good chick health. Freshly hatched chicks can benefit from electrolytes but they should not be provided for more than 5 consecutive days. Chicks should be only be fed the medicated Purina Start & Grow that is fortified with probiotics and Amprolium for coccidiosis protection. The starter can be fed until a Peacock is full grown but 3 to 4 months is the recommended minimum. Chicks can be taken off the medicated Purina Start & Grow at 3 to 4 months and converted to a flock raiser crumble. Turkey, Peacocks, Pheasants and other game birds will develop their resistance to coccidiosis by 3 to 4 months. There are those who have other ideas about what to feed their chicks. But you cannot go wrong with the medicated Purina Start & Grow found at Tractor Supply and other Purina dealers. However, you can go wrong with starters and feeds blended up at home. When medicated starters are mixed with other feeds, the therapeutic level of the Amprolium ingredient to combat Coccidiosis is compromised. The medicated Purina Start & Grow must be a 90% minimum of everything fed to your chicks in order to maintain a therapeutic level of Amprolium that combats Coccidiosis.

More than any other kind of chick, peachicks crave heat. The proper way to insure they have enough heat is to lay a thermometer flat under the heat lamp. You can keep it at 90 to 95 degrees by either raising or lowering the lamp or by adjusting the light bulb wattage. Be sure your coop or brooder has enough space for the chicks to find their comfort zone. The mistake many make is to bring the chicks inside into the air conditioning. Then put a heat lamp down into a cardboard box or a where there is no ventilation. Or, worse yet, no heat lamp at all is provided. Some are keeping peacocks of different ages in the bathtub, in the shower stall or giving them the run of the bathroom. This is just not healthy for peacocks of any age. Build a coop off the ground under a shelter and provide a heat lamp. Do not turn the heat off because you believe the weather is too hot. You can adjust the lamp height and wattage to address that. A peacock's temperature is 104 to 105. A 90 degree ambient temperature is something different to for them. If you do not provide heat for your chicks, one day you will be asking "why are all of my chicks gasping and dying?"

ALL STARTER FEEDS ARE NOT CREATED EQUAL

By: Doug Buffington

When comparing different feeds it is important to take note of more than the level of Crude Protein at the top of the ingredient list on the tag. The Synthetic amino acids Lysine and Methionine should also be under review. These are the "enhanced" proteins that accelerate growth. Many feed producers set their starter feed levels at the maximum of 1.5% for Lysine and Methionine at .5%. The protein levels of some will reach 30%. Peachicks cannot be fed high protein starters without risking an over growth that will cause developmental problems from leg and toe overgrowths. A number of them will begin to develop slipped tendons that are not repairable. Those who claim to feed high protein starters without problems are just lucky.

Many are not aware of the risk of chick overgrowth. Others who are aware of overgrowth often feed other rations that are not medicated for Coccidiosis. They have the misguided notion that the FDA approved medicated starters will kill chicks. The immune systems of Peacocks, Pheasant, Turkeys and other game birds are not fully developed to resist Coccidiosis until they reach the age of 3 to 4 months. So, chicks often go unprotected for the period required for a full immune system development. During this period, people who feed unmedicated and high protein starters begin to wonder why their chicks are dying and why the legs and toes are crippling them.

A favored starter is the medicated, 18% protein Purina Start & Grow. The levels of Protein, Lysine and Methionine are adjusted so that the medicated ration may be fed until they reach the 3 to 4 month minimum and beyond without the risk of chick overgrowth. The first 3 months of a medicated starter will allow the immune system of your chicks to achieve their maximum resistance to Coccidiosis. Some breeders are feeding it for the first year until the Peacocks are full grown. But medicated starters need to be fed for a minimum of 3 to 4 months before converting to a Flock Raiser crumble. Consider keeping all peacock feed as a crumble.

There are other benefits of feeding the Purina Start & Grow that are yet to be observed in other starter rations. Not only are the levels of protein, Methionine and Lysine adjusted so the ration can be safely fed for the 3 to 4 month minimum but the Purina Start & Grow also has added Probiotics and Prebiotics. They are microorganisms that support the growth, health and immune system development of chicks.

Another advantage of the constant presence of Probiotics and Prebiotics in the starter feed is that they will more quickly restore a chick's immune system after the use of antibiotics.

HERE IS THE TAKE AWAY on the Purina Start & Grow.

1. The crude protein level is 18% and recommended as the only feed for a minimum of 3 to 4 months.
2. The amino acids Lysine and Methionine are adjusted to safely sustain growth to allow the maximum development of the immune system while the Amprolium protects against Coccidiosis.
3. Probiotics and Prebiotics are added to Start & Grow to promote health, growth and immune system development.

Remember, it is the Purina Medicated Start & Grow that you want to feed. What many peacock breeders fail to grasp is that a 30% protein Game Bird Starter is for release and shoot Pheasants that growers want to speed to the field and before the shotguns in the shortest time possible. And, we are not trying to speed the peacock to the Thanksgiving table. Feeding a non-mediated, high protein Game Bird Starter leaves the peachick unprotected against Coccidiosis and risks poor leg and toe development. Non-medicated starters are for waterfowl. Ducklings are not susceptible to coccidiosis. Also, the proper development of ducklings will require the 3 to 4% more niacin that is added to non-medicated starters.

SWITCHING YOUNG PEACOCKS FROM A STARTER CRUMBLE TO A PELLET...... Converting juvenile peacocks from a crumble to a pellet is not always successful. Some will starve out with even the smallest pellet because it is too hard for them to swallow. A good solution is to convert from a medicated starter crumble to the Purina Flock Raiser crumble found at Tractor Supply or at any Purina dealer. A chick will acquire its full immune resistance to Coccidiosis after 3 months of medicated starter. The conversion can be made any time after 3 months. Eventually, the peacocks will need to be converted to the 18% Purina Gamebird Layer crumble during the laying season and back to a Flock Raiser after the season. Feeding crumbles will eliminate the problems with feed conversion from one type to another.

BUYING "FERTILE" PEACOCK EGGS
by: Doug Buffington

Often, people express an interest in buying "fertile" eggs. There are a number of things to be considered before acquiring these eggs.

To begin, there is no way to buy fertile eggs because there is no way to test fertility before the sale. What is being purchased are eggs that may be fertile and that may hatch if they are. Peacock eggs are notorious for infertiles and quitters (eggs that partially develop before quitting). Then there are those that fully develop but refuse to hatch.

Peacock eggs do not incubate well. No matter how perfectly they are incubated, the rate of hatch failure is higher than that of chickens and other poultry eggs. A poor hatch rate combined with the number of infertile eggs makes the cost of surviving chicks very expensive. Sometimes chicks can be purchased for less than the cost of the eggs to produce them when all costs and the hatch rate are factored in.

In addition to a poor hatch rate of incubated eggs, there are other factors that can contribute to hatching failures. One factor is how the eggs are stored before the sale. Properly stored eggs are kept at a temperature of 60 degrees and 60% humidity while being turned twice daily. Even the hatch rate of properly kept eggs will begin to diminish after 7 days. It is unlikely that many egg sellers observe the proper storage requirements or even know how old their eggs are before shipping.

Another factor that contributes to the hatch rate failure is the manner of shipping. Some shippers do not provide the packing necessary to absorb the bumps and vibration of transport. Additionally, the temperatures that eggs are exposed to are a great unknown. How much cold are they exposed to and how much heat? Both can be lethal to fertile eggs.

One more thing…eggs laid at one altitude should be incubated at approximately the same altitude. The number of pores in the eggshell will allow more or less oxygen to enter and moisture to escape. The number of pores will vary by altitude. Keep this in mind when you order eggs. Those purchased at sea level should not be incubated at altitudes of a half-mile or more.

Lastly, the color or color pattern of a peacock from a purchased egg is not perfectly predictable. Peacocks are often carrying a number of recessive genes for color and color patterns. You may get what you paid for and you may not.

DISEASES OF PEAFOWL

by: Dr. L. Dwight Schwartz, DVM

There is an aura of mystique about diseases and illnesses that are common to ornamental birds, hobby birds, zoos, and exotic birds. Peafowl would certainly be included in this group of birds.

The peafowl, Pavo Cristatus, is a bird about the size of a turkey, Meleagridis gallopavo. Peafowl are Old World birds originating in India and Sri-Lanka while the turkey is a New World bird being a native of North America. Other than being continents apart, the two species are quite similar and actually somewhat related. However, the diet of the peafowl in the wild (Asia) is snails, frogs, insects, grains, juicy grasses, and bulbs which is somewhat different from the birds in this country (US).

The peafowl is the showiest of all birds because of its size and the beauty of its train. The male bird, the peacock, is the showy bird of the species while the peahen is smaller with less varied colors and lacks the long train. The peafowl has been treasured for its great beauty since Biblical times (I Kings 10:22). About 400 B.C., royalty in Rome considered peafowl a great delicacy as a roast and served in its own feathers. The best known of this bird family is the Indian peafowl, India's national bird, and is also the primary peafowl in America.

The diseases of peafowl are almost identical to those of its New World counterpart, the turkey. Likewise, peafowl will respond to medications that are known to be effective for the turkey. This is to say that anyone experiencing illness in peafowl can consider it a turkey when seeking diagnosis and establishing a treatment.

Infectious diseases of peafowl across the whole spectrum of etiological or causative agents including virus, virus-like bacteria, fungi, protozoan, worms, and external parasites. Similarly, all systems of the bird are affected by these infections. The approaches to study diseases are to consider specific infections, regardless of causative agent by systems such as the respiratory, digestive, immune, reproductive, circulatory, renal, and nervous systems. The more common approach is to study the disease agent by its manifestations, clinical signs, systems affected, and control. One soon learns by disease name what system(s) will be affected.

The Poultry Health Handbook uses both of these approaches. Section II covers respiratory diseases while subsequent sections cover diseases by category of the causative agent such as virus, bacteria, protozoa, internal and external parasites. The experienced peafowl and poultry breeder become familiar with diseases endemic on their farm, locality, or state.

All bird fanciers are encouraged to familiarize themselves with necropsy (post-mortem) procedures and should routinely necropsy freshly dead or sick birds at the onset of a disease outbreak. Even if you contact your veterinarian or the birds are submitted to a diagnostic laboratory, you need to be in a position to describe the lesions you found in the birds.

Important points to observe are the feathering, fleshing, the color of flesh, scaly legs, crusts on beak or eyelids, internal lesions by organ, i.e. heart liver, lungs, spleen, intestine, gonads, and kidney.

There are approximately 80 infectious diseases that are somewhat regularly diagnosed in peafowl. Luckily, only a few of these are found in any given flock; therefore, the producers should be familiar with the diseases in his or her own flock. This further emphasizes the importance of early recognition of the common problems in your flock. Every acute disease episode should be confirmed with a laboratory diagnosis.

A common question that I am often asked is, "What tests should I do on my birds?" A relevant answer is the tests that are outlined in the National Poultry Improvement Program (NPIP). The program focuses on diseases that should be eradicated: Salmonella Pullorum (Pullorum) and S. gallinarum (Fowl Typhoid). Since there is no cure for these diseases, the program requires an annual blood test. The producer can be trained to conduct this simple test on the farm. I recommend that each fall as you select breeding stock for the coming year that you pullorum test the birds. Keep the tested birds separate from the birds that you do not plan to keep. The annual test of flocks participating in the NPIP program qualifies the birds for exhibition and interstate travel without further tests at the time of show or export. Keep the forms that show the birds are negative as proof of the tests as well as the bird being negative for pullorum and fowl typhoid. The one test, Whole Blood Plate Agglutination, detects both diseases. Every peafowl breeder should be a participant in the NPIP Program.

Now a brief dissertation on the most common diseases in the peafowl is divided into categories.

VIRUS AND VIRUS-LIKE DISEASES

Newcastle Disease (ND) is an acute rapidly-spreading respiratory disease that is caused by a virus. ND can cause high mortality depending on the virulence or pathogenicity of the virus. The duration of ND is about 14 days. Since there is no effective medication against ND, it must be prevented or controlled by a vaccination accompanied by excellent husbandry at all times.

Fowl Pox (FP) is a relatively slow-spreading disease caused by a virus that is transmitted primarily via the bite of infected mosquitoes. The poxvirus replicates or reproduces in the epithelial tissue; hence lesions are confined to unfathered areas of the skin, conjunctiva of the eye, and throat area. Fowl Pox is a true pox in that the lesions are raised, scabby, and crater-like with the scab firmly attached until the lesion is healed. Treatment would include vaccination of flock before or during an outbreak, mosquito control, and topical treatment of pox lesions with a skin antiseptic.

Hemorrhagic Enteritis (HE) is an acute and often fatal disorder caused by an adenovirus. The disease is characterized by extensive inflammation and hemorrhage of the intestines. The birds are most susceptible between 4 and 13 weeks of age. The disease is not spread bird to bird but from the ingestion of infected material such as fecal droppings in the feed, water, or litter. Prevention by sound management and vaccination is the best policy since there is no specific treatment. However; antibiotics in the feed or water are a good therapy to prevent a secondary infection which would shorten the recovery period.

M. gallisepticum (MG), M. synoviae (MS), and M. meleagridis (MM) are mycoplasma diseases with MG and MM being the most serious and prevalent. Both MG and MM produce respiratory illness often diagnosed or reported as "Sinusitis", swelling of the eye sinuses, and "Air Sacculitis", air sacs or air reservoirs of the respiratory system are inflamed and contain exudates or pus. MS infections are seen as arthritic and joint infections. There are no absolute cures for mycoplasma infections but several antibiotics are effective as treatment and control of the infections. Recovered peafowl remain carriers and the disease is transmitted from the hen to the chick in the egg. Therefore; it is best not to save any mycoplasma positive birds for breeding purposes since this would be perpetuating the disease year after year.

BACTERIAL DISEASES

Pullorum and Fowl typhoid are acute diseases caused by bacteria of the genus Salmonella — S. pullorum and S. gallinarum, respectively. These two bacteria are antigenically related. Both are spread from infected breeder birds to the progeny in the egg. To control these diseases, blood test the parent birds before the breeding season and eliminate the Pullorum-positive birds. If all Pullorum-positive birds are destroyed, all progeny would be pullorum and typhoid free.

Paratyphoid is an acute septicemic and intestinal disease caused by a bacterium of the genus Salmonella. There are at least 2000 serotypes in this bacterial group which makes control by testing of the parent bird unfeasible. Paratyphoid causes high mortality in young birds from 8 to 28 days. After that, infected birds are chronically ill with many becoming stunned and unthrifty. Like pullorum and fowl typhoid, paratyphoid is spread from the infected hen to the chick. Chicks become infected at hatching as they come in contact with bacteria on contaminated egg shells. Losses from paratyphoid can be reduced by medication, neomycin or nitrofuran, in the chick starter feed.

Arizona (paracolon) infection is an acute septicemic and intestinal infection in young birds. Arizona infections parallels paratyphoid in seriousness, losses and disease symptoms. The Arizona bacterium is closely related to Salmonella; therefore, isolation and identification procedures are identical. Differentiation between Arizona and paratyphoid should be made in any outbreak because of the close relationship between the two pathogens. Arizona is sensitive to drugs used for paratyphoid. Neomycin and/or nitrofuran drugs are recommended for treatment and control.

Staphylococcus is an infectious non-contagious disease caused by a bacterium Staphylococcus aureus. The disease is characterized by septicemia, bumble foot and/or arthritis. Staphylococci are ubiquitous with most infections contracted by birds individually from the environment. Outbreaks do respond to antibiotic therapy that can be administered to birds individually or to the flock in the feed or water. Improved sanitation of the housing environment and better flock management will help control staphylococcosis.

Fowl Cholera (FC) is an acute septicemic infection caused by the bacterium Pasteurella multocida. The disease is characterized by a rather sudden onset, high mortality with extensive hemorrhages in affected birds. The best control is prevention of the introduction of Pasteurella into the flock from new birds, sick birds, or contaminated materials and equipment. Vaccines are commercially available but are only marginally successful.

Outbreaks can be brought under control by flock medication with sulfa drugs and antibiotics. Premises will remain infected following a FC outbreak unless a thorough decontamination program is conducted.

Avian tuberculosis (TB) is a slow spreading disease of adult birds, probably 3 to 4 years of age in peafowl. The disease is caused by the bacterium Mycobacterium avian, an acid-fast organism. TB is characterized by gradual emaciation with the development of Tubercles (granulomas) in the viscera and is contracted by the bird from the infected environment. Infected premises remain infected for long periods unless there is a deliberate decontamination program developed. To confirm a diagnosis, the acid-fast staining technique is used. There is no treatment against TB. Improved management, better sanitation of the environment will help to prevent the introduction of the disease.

PROTOZOAN DISEASES

Coccidiosis is an infection caused by one or more species of coccidia. Avian coccidia protozoan organism belongs to the genus Elmeria. Coccidia is a disease primarily of young birds 3 to 12 weeks of age. Coccidia is host specific; that is, coccidia does not cross infect from one bird species to another. Most bird species are subject to coccidial infection by 2 or more species. Coccidiosis is best controlled by preventative medication in the feed during the susceptible age of the birds. Coccidiostats (preventive drugs) are available commercially with Amprolium and Rofenaid being the most prominent two. If a coccidiostat cannot be obtained, any good sulfa drug can be substituted in the feed. When outbreaks occur, birds can be treated with sulfa drugs in the drinking water. All drugs should be used in accordance with the label instructions.

Histomoniasis, commonly called "Blackhead" is an infectious intestinal disease caused by the protozoa Histomonas meleagridis. Birds are most susceptible between 6 and 14 weeks of age. Symptoms are watery, sulfur-colored droppings, drowsiness, and weakness. The causative agent is shed in the feces of the infected birds and then contracted by susceptible birds as they feed from the floor and litter. Histomoniasis can be controlled by specific medication of a bird or flock at the onset of an outbreak or prevented with the use of a histomonastat, drug specific from Histomoniasis, in the feed. Presently there are no FDA approved Histomonastats. Currently, Metronidazole (Flagyl), copper sulfate, and Histostat are the medications used for the treatment of Blackhead.

Trichomoniasis is a disease found especially in young birds. There are two forms of this disease: (1) Mouth, crop-esophagus infection or upper form caused by Trichomonas gallinae and (2) Intestinal or lower form caused by Trichomonas gallinarum. Birds with the upper form will be depressed, drool, have a sunken empty crop, swallow frequently and have a fetid odor. Many affected birds will maintain an upright penguin-like body posture. Signs of the lower form are depression, unthriftiness, loss of weight, and yellow-watery diarrhea. The symptoms are similar to Histomoniasis with treatment and control the same as for Histomoniasis.

Leucocytozoonosis is a malaria-like disease caused by a protozoan organism that parasitizes the white blood cells of the bird host. This disease is world-wide in distribution and occurs regionally in a nation or country where situations are conducive for the vectors to breed. Birds of any age are susceptible but are the most devastating in the young birds. The disease is most prevalent in birds on range. Onset is sudden with severe anemia, fever, weakness, loss of appetite, and lameness. In the terminal stages of the disease, birds will vomit, excrete green feces, and die. Leucocytozoonosis is transmitted by infected vectors, blackflies (Simuliuim sp.) and biting midges (Culicoidos sp.). Both vectors breed in fast flowing streams. Prevention is by keeping susceptible birds confined to buildings during the vector season. Neither of these insect vectors will feed inside buildings; hence, confinement prevents exposure. Treatment of birds during outbreaks will be a sulfa drug or clopidol (Coyden) will bring the disease under control.

Haemoproteus infection or pigeon malaria is caused by a protozoan blood parasite of the genus Haemonproteus that invades and destroys the red blood cells. This results in severe anemia and death of the bird. Haemoproteus is transmitted by blood sucking insects including the biting midge (Culicoides) as described with Leucocytozoonosis. The disease onset is sudden with general weakness, lethargy, poor appetite, and death. Antimalaria drugs are effective against Haemoproteus for treatment of outbreaks. Prevention can be by a combination of insect control and a low-level continuous medication with an antimalarial drug or Clopidol.

INTERNAL PARASITES

Ascaridia, common roundworms, are prevalent in many species of fowl. Ascarid species are essentially host specific in that each has its preferred bird species. The ascarid life cycle is egg-larva-adult. The worm egg is passed in the feces, germinates on the environment, and is then eaten by a susceptible host which provides opportunity to complete the life cycle. The larva migrates extensively in the intestinal lining causing much tissue damage, blood loss, intestinal lesions with complications. Adult worms are susceptible to piperazine worm medicine that can be administered in the water or moist feed for a one-day treatment. Medication can be periodically repeated as needed.

Cecal Worms, Heterakis gallinea, are tiny worms that live in the ceca (blind pouches) of the birds. These worms cause little damage or discomfort to the bird but are important because they serve in the perpetuation of histomoniasis. The dormant histomonad has been shown to exist from one season to the next in the egg of the cecal worm. The flock can be dewormed effectively with one of several commercially available wormers.

Gapeworms, Syngamus trachea, are worms that localize in the trachea (windpipe) of birds. Heavy infections cause respiratory distress in young birds with their small trachea being mechanically blocked which plugs the passage of air. Infective Syngamus eggs apparently winter over in worm-contaminated pens. It is also thought that earthworms are an intermediate host of this parasite. Control is treatment of infected birds with Thiabendazole or Tramisol.

Capillaria worms, capillaria sp. are parasites of the gastro-intestinal tract. At least two capillaria species are known to infect the crop, esophagus, and mouth while other species (4 or 5) localize in the intestine and ceca. Each species tends to have its preferred location in the digestive tract. Capillaria cause a general unthriftiness, paleness and rough feather coat in the infected birds. Capillaria are resistant to most poultry wormers; however, Thiabendazole, Tramisol, Fenbandazole, or Ivermactin would be recommended.

Tapeworms (numerous species) are known to parasitize fowl. It is assumed that only those species common to the peafowl and/or turkeys would be involved. Tapeworms have a two-stage lifecycle with the bird being the second stage or the primary host. The first stage occurs in insects, arthropods, and crustaceans called secondary hosts. Peafowls become infected from feeding on infected secondary hosts. Symptoms usually depend on finding tapeworm segments in the bird feces. Periodic treatment of the birds will free them of tapeworms but reinfection usually begins again as the peafowl returns to the source of the infected secondary host.

EXTERNAL PARASITES

Lice are common external parasites in outdoor birds and birds in the wild. Lice are insects that spend their entire life cycle on the host. Lice feed on skin, scales, and feather debris. Poultry lice have chewing mouthparts. Lice spread from bird to bird as body contact is made by birds. Control is established by initiation treatment for all birds in the flock on a periodic basis with an approved safe pesticide. Treatment is not recommended unless lice are present on the birds.

Mites are common to all avian species. The Northern mite is the most prevalent and troublesome of the mites in poultry and other birds. Mites are members of the spider family. They spend their entire life cycle on the bird and tend to be more resistant than lice to pesticides. Mites spread from bird to bird as flock members make body contact. The life cycle is 7 to 14 days so control requires treatment at 10-day intervals for 3 to 4 treatments and monthly thereafter of all birds in the flock with an approved safe pesticide.

Chiggers are mites that live and reproduce in the environment. The chigger that parasitizes birds and mammals represents the nymphal, or immature stage of the mite. Chiggers feed in clusters on the thighs, breast, undersides of the wings, and the vent. These chigger clusters result in reddish scabby lesions. The chiggers feed for about 14 days, then drop off after which the lesion heals. Control would require the treatment of the pen or range inhabited by the bird.

NUTRITIONAL DISEASES

These diseases result from a deficiency in the diet of essential required vitamins or minerals. Nutritional disorders most often seen in young birds are:

1. Rickets – Calcium, phosphorus, vitamin D deficiency

2. Curled Toe Paralysis – Riboflavin deficiency

3. Nutritional Roup – Vitamin A deficiency

4. Perosis – Manganese deficiency

5. Crazy Chick Disease – Vitamin E deficiency

6. Gizzard Myopathy (white muscle disease) – Selenium deficiency

Treatment requires the correction of the deficiency in the feed plus a short period of vitamin-electrolyte supplementation in the water.

DOUG'S BITS & PIECES

FOR PEACOCKS AND PEACHICKS

1. Let chicks stay in the incubator for 3 days until they are active and standing strong. They will not need to eat or drink for these 3 days.
2. Keep chicks on wire off the ground for the first 4 months.
3. Feed a medicated starter only of not more than 20% protein. Medicated starters must be 90% of a chick's diet to remain therapeutic for coccidiosis. Allow chicks enough space to exercise.
4. Keep a heat lamp on the chicks until they are let out on the ground at 4 months. You can adjust the heat as needed by raising and lowering the lamp or changing the wattage of the bulb.
5. Chicks will not need worming for the first couple of months on the ground at the soonest.
6. A blue neck on a male chick will first be green.
7. It takes 4 months for a chick's immune system to develop its resistance to coccidiosis and blackhead.
8. Have a proper coop set up outside with a heat lamp for the chicks. A coop under a shed without a draft is even better.
9. Young chicks can be treated with the All in One medication if they are drinking normally to take up a therapeutic dose.
10. "Free range" peacocks will eventually sour relations with the neighbors by crapping on their cars, digging in their garden and keeping them up all night. Be a good neighbor.
11. Free range peacocks will often leave and not come back…ever.
12. You cannot free range on two acres of land. Your peacocks will never learn where the boundaries are.
13. For goodness sakes, build some fence at least 5' tall and put a shelter in it with feeding stations and keep your coops in it too.
14. Young peacocks raised behind the fence of a spacious pen will tend to remain behind it. A fence of 5' is often enough.
15. Medicated starter feeds will not kill chicks.

16. Feeding a peacock is not a science experiment. Do not blend up a hodgepodge of this and that. You cannot possibly know more than the PhD's at the major feed mills.
17. Buy the Purina Start & Grow, Flock Raiser and Game Bird Layer. Feeding a peacock is really just that simple.
18. If you want treats, buy a 50lb bag of whole kernel corn. It is cheap and the peacocks will love it. Anything more is feeding your own psychology.
19. Please keep medications on hand. A number of the best medications can only be ordered online. Your sick bird does not have the time to wait on the mail.
20. If you are using Corid to treat your sick peacocks, there are way better products out there.
21. A small splash of apple cider vinegar will keep chick water fresh longer. But it is not a medicine that will cure any type of disease. Do not put it in a metal container. It will eat the galvanize off of it.
22. If you have a sick bird, get some real medicine. Stop trying to treat it with vinegar and kitchen spices.
23. Scratch grains have the nutritional value of pea gravel.
24. Feed some corn to your birds in the fall and winter to fatten them up a little. Offer it free choice along with whatever else you are feeding.
25. Worm your birds at least before and after the laying season. Every 3 to 4 months if they are kept in proximity to chickens.
26. Penned peacocks will require more vigilance and medications must be kept on hand. They will keep reinfecting themselves with worms, coccidiosis and blackhead as well as respiratory infections.
27. Anything recommended for peacocks can be applied to all farm birds.
28. The All in One medication can be used to treat any bird from a canary to an ostrich.
29. Young chicks brought into the house or garage will too often get sick and die.
30. Do not raise chicks in pet carriers. It's just wrong.
31. "Save a Chick" from tractor supply is good for perking chicks up, especially after a transfer. Do not provide it for more than 5 days in a row. Mix it up fresh daily. The same for All in One.

32. Over the counter antibiotic salve is good to treat young chicks with eye problems.
33. Get chicks to eat by placing a starter feed on a double layer of paper towel with water nearby. It will trigger the pecking instinct. They do not need a "teacher chick" to tell them they are hungry. However, they typically do not eat or drink for the first three days.
34. Do not make hand raised pets out of your chicks. When they are older they have a hard time figuring out what part of the flock you are and begin to attack you and the kids.
35. Peacocks do not need a feed with a protein level higher than the 20% found in a Flock Raiser. Trust me.
36. Never feed a peachick anything that says game bird or turkey on the label if it is more than 18 or 20% protein. It will cause your chicks to overgrow and develop crippling leg and toe problems.
37. The All in One is not a preventative. It is a medicine for birds that are symptomatic of an illness. Do not use it for routine worming.
38. Worm medications must be followed by another dose 10 to 12 days after the end of the first treatment. This catches the worm eggs left behind that have hatched since the first round. However, Ivermectin and Moxivet plus do not require a follow-up dose.
39. Rotate worm medications to prevent resistance from developing.
40. If your peacocks roost in the trees, they will need a daytime shelter with feeding stations for rainy days and when it snows.
41. Peacock pens can never be too large…only too small.
42. Set your feeders on blocks. Hanging them is even better. Feeders will need to be moved from time to time to prevent bacteria buildup on the ground.
43. Never buy birds from the auction. They will be full of worms, sick or crippled… or all three. Would you buy a used car at an auction?
44. Quarantine and give an All-in-One treatment to every new bird that comes to your place and treat every bird that leaves your place too. It is a good practice and a good selling point.
45. Build some coops, shelters, and fences. Do not keep chicks in the house until you believe they are old enough to throw out the back door to "free range" the neighborhood.
46. Help new owners learn how to feed and medicate peacocks every chance you get.

Intramuscular Medication Dosing of Peafowl

by: Craig Hopkins

Many peafowl medications are most effective when given intramuscularly. An intramuscular dose of medication assures that the peafowl are getting the proper dose and that no bird has missed getting the medication. When peafowl are showing signs of illness, there is no better way to get them on the road to recovery than to give them the medication directly into their breast muscle. While intramuscular dosing has many advantages, it must be done properly to assure that the bird gets the full benefit of the medication and is not injured during the process. The purpose of this article is to describe and illustrate the proper method of giving an intramuscular dose of medication to peafowl. The steps described in this article can be done by one or two people.

The first step in this process is to catch the peafowl and to properly restrain them so that they do not injure themselves or you. I use a large fishing net with a long retractable handle to catch the bird. The net material is not the normal coarsely woven nylon mesh. I use a tightly woven nylon mesh made especially for catching birds. Entire nets or just the mesh material can be purchased from most poultry or pheasant supply companies. Once the bird is caught, pin the bird to the ground with the net and grasp both legs firmly with a gloved hand.

It is best to grasp both legs at the knee joint and to hold both legs in one hand. Remove the bird from the net and cradle it against your body so that it cannot flap its wings.

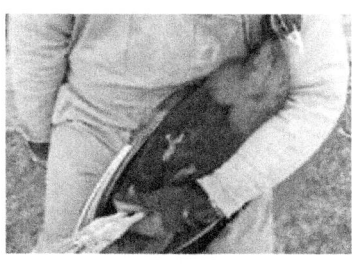
The second step is to hold the bird in such a way as to allow for the injection to be given in the breast muscle. If two people are participating, hold the bird on its back in your lap. Continue to hold the legs at the knee joint and secure the wings against your body and with your free hand. If you are working by yourself, hold the bird on its back in your lap. Hold the feet at the knee and secure the wings with your hand and arm. Your free hand will be needed to administer the injection. I am right-handed so reverse the bird's position if you are left-handed.

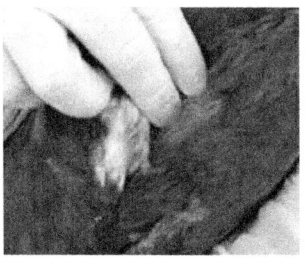
The next step is to locate the breast muscle. This can be done by running your fingers along the breastbone and then feeling on either side of the breastbone. In a healthy bird, the breast bone will feel dull to the touch and the muscle will be nice and firm. In a sick bird, the breast muscle will feel very sharp and the muscle will be very small and hard to distinguish.

Be careful in this scenario not to hit the bone with the needle and possibly break it off. Once the breast muscle has been found, insert the needle at a 45-degree angle to the muscle and inject the medication. If repeated injections are required to cure the bird, it is a good idea to alternate the injections on both sides of the breast bone.

I use 3cc syringes with 20-gauge needles to dose most medications. The needles are ¾" in length. This length of the needle helps to prevent going too deep with the needle and penetrating through the muscle. An insulin syringe works well for small doses and on young peafowl. Once the proper syringe has been selected and the proper dose of medication has been drawn into the syringe, you are ready to medicate your bird.

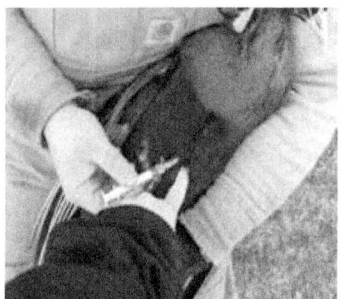

Once the syringe is empty, remove it from the bird's breast and apply light pressure where the shot has been placed for 15 seconds. The bird can now be released.

Heated Roost for Peafowl

by: Craig Hopkins

hopkinslivestock.com

In many areas of the country where wintertime temperatures drop well below freezing, there is a need for providing a heated roost for cold-sensitive varieties of peafowl and game birds. We live in east-central Indiana and we provide a heated roost for our Burmese green peafowl. The heated roost design that is described in this article is very inexpensive to build and to operate during periods of sub-freezing weather. We use this heated roost only for our Burmese green peafowl, but it can be used with any variety and age of peafowl to prevent frostbitten toes and to reduce deaths caused by extremely cold weather. The bill of materials required can be found at the end of this article. Roosts for peafowl should always be placed so that the peafowl sit on the flat side of a 2" x 4" or 2" x 6".

This allows the peafowl to sit on their feet, rather than with their toes exposed while gripping a round roost, which prevents frostbitten toes.

If the roost bows due to the number of roosting peafowl or the length of the roost or both, a second 2" x 4" will have to be installed on the edge on the bottom side of the roost to provide added support.

Step 1: Purchase an electric heat tape used on water pipes to prevent them from freezing. <u>The heat tape should have a thermostat that will turn it off and on at approximately 38 F</u>. The heat tape should be long enough to run along the 2" x 4" twice. Leave about 6" of each end of the 2" x 4" uncovered by the heat tape so the completed roost can be secured inside of the building or stall. This will reduce the length of the heat tape required by 1'. See photo #1

Step 2: Secure the heat tape to the flat side of the 2" x 4" with the plastic staples. Be sure to leave enough excess heat tape on the thermostat end so that the thermostat can hang freely under the roost.

This prevents the peafowl from sitting on the thermostat and giving it an inaccurate reading of the actual air temperature. See photos #2, 3

Step 3: Wrap the carpeting around the roost and secure it to the bottom side of the 2" x 4" with roofing nails or long staples. Leave about 4" on each end of the roost uncovered by the carpet. The roost is now complete. See photo #4

Step 4: Install the roost with drywall screws or nails. I use drywall screws so that the roost can be removed once the cold weather months have passed.

Bill of material:

1) 1, 2" x 4" x length required for roost.

2) 1, electric heat tape with thermostat. 110 volt, 2x length of 2" x 4" minus 1'.

3) Plastic staples used for 12/2 electric wire. Space every 2' to secure heat tape.

4) Carpet remnant or piece of indoor/outdoor carpeting to wrap the 2" x 4" and heat tape.

5) 1 ¼" roofing nails spaced every 1' to secure carpeting to 2" x 4".

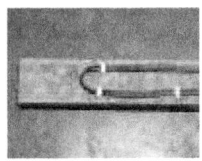 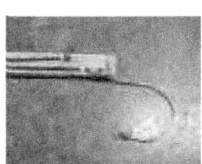 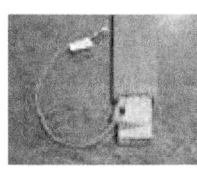 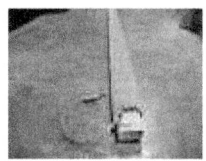

Photo #1   Photo #2   Photo #3   Photo #4

Swelling of the Eye Sinuses

by: Craig Hopkins

Hopkins' Alternative Livestock does not accept any responsibility for the use of this information by those other than Hopkins' Alternative Livestock.

I receive many phone calls and emails throughout the year describing peafowl that has swelling of the eye sinuses. The severity of the swelling can range from just some puffiness below the eye to an eye that is so swollen that it is on the verge of bursting. I would like to use this article to help peafowl breeders treat this problem and more importantly prevent it from happening in the first place.

I have helped fellow breeders with this problem during all seasons of the year but late summer and fall seem to be a common time for peafowl to have this illness. My own experience was during the late summer. A friend of mine was keeping some of my surplus breeders at his house. In the pen next to the peafowl were a dozen guineas. The guineas were on a cement floor with straw bedding. Guineas love to scratch through their bedding and they generate a lot of dust. Within a couple of weeks, the first peacock showed signs of swelling in the soft tissue below the eye. A second peahen had swelling the next day. Both of these birds were isolated and given medications in their drinking water. Two different medicines were given and neither medication reduced the swelling. A week had passed for the first peacock and his eye sinus was now swollen to about half the size of a ping-pong ball. The peacock also would cough and shake his head to try to get rid of excess mucus in his beak and throat.

I decided to try Tylan 200 on these birds since Tylan 200 has proven to be very effective for me in treating any respiratory problem. Both birds were given 2cc in the breast muscle using a 3cc syringe and an 18-gauge needle. Within a day the swelling was gone in the peahen and the swelling was almost gone in the peacock. A second shot two days after the first shot brought the peacock's eye sinus back to normal and cleared up the excess mucous.

I chose to treat this problem like a respiratory illness because of the swelling in the eye sinuses and the excess mucous in the throat. I also observed that the second pen of peafowl, in a separate building away from the guineas and the dust, never were affected.

Once I determined that the illness was being caused by the dust stirred up by the guineas, the guineas and peafowl were placed in separate buildings. The dusty pens were completely cleaned out and disinfected with Tek-trol. The pens were allowed to dry out for a day and clean straw bedding was placed in the pens. I have kept peafowl in these pens without any further illness problems. I have made it a standard procedure to spray down all pens with Tek-trol after all of the old bedding has been removed.

In the years that have passed since my own experience with this illness, I have helped dozens of peafowl breeders treat birds with the same symptoms. The common thread between all of these breeders has been that the peafowl was being kept in a dusty environment. The excess dust can be caused by guineas, chickens, too many peafowls in a given space, poor ventilation, moldy bedding, and fine, dusty feed. The dry, dusty conditions of late summer and fall in many areas seem to make this illness more prevalent as well.

There are several diseases that can cause similar symptoms in peafowl and poultry. There is an excellent listing of diseases and their symptoms on the UPA website www.peafowl.org. If peafowl do not respond to the treatment described earlier, I would take the birds to a vet. Baytril is another drug that is very effective for respiratory illnesses but it has to be prescribed by a vet. I chose to use Tylan 200 because I have had excellent results with it. Tylan 200 is a cattle antibiotic and it is not labeled for use on peafowl so use it with this understanding.

If the eye sinuses are severely swollen and have been for several days, you may have to have a vet lance the swollen area once the swelling goes down because the fluid has hardened and will not go down completely to normal size.

GAPING BIRD DIAGNOSIS AND TREATMENT

by: Doug Buffington

A gaping/gasping peacock exhibits a "yawning" action. The more frequent the action, the more critical the condition. Gaping is something that must be treated without any delay.

There are 4 conditions that can result in a gaping and gasping peacock.

1. **OBSTRUCTION**--- open the bird's mouth to look for some type of foreign body like string or plastic in the trachea and throat. TREATMENT… The removal will depend on the obstruction but most commonly, tweezers will remove it.
2. **RESPIRATORY INFECTION**--- gaping and gasping can be caused by a respiratory infection. Symptoms will often include a runny nose, swollen sinuses or labored breathing. TREATMENT… A 2cc intramuscular injection of Tylan 200 or 3/4cc injections of LA 200 (SubQ) will clear up the infection. Give one injection daily of either for 3 to 4 days. LA 200 is Oxytetracycline that is also sold under the brand names of Duramycin 72-200, Liquamycin and others. Two or three 1cc injections of Baytril 100 is also highly effective. Tylan 200 should be given in the muscle of the leg or breast. Oxytetracycline (LA 200) and Baytril 100 can be injected under the skin pulled up at the base and back of the neck closer to where the wings begin. Oxytetracycline can be given as an injection, drench or fed directly onto a piece of bread or over some dry dog or cat food. Be careful not use Oxytetracycline in combination with the All in One medication or Ronidazole 20%. Oxytetracycline will conflict with the Ronidazole.
3. **CANKER**---these are protozoan white to yellow growths found in the beak, on the tongue and around the trachea of peafowl and other farm birds. Left untreated, they will grow to where your birds can not eat, drink or even breath. It can be treated with the All in

One medication in combination with two 250mg metronidazole tablets daily for 10 days to two weeks or Ronidazole 20% added to the drinking water if an infected bird is drinking normally. However, it must be remembered that these are only treatments and may not be a complete cure. Infected peafowl must be segregated and medicated with follow up treatments. They should not be penned with uninfected farm birds or other peafowl or free ranged with them. When treating for Canker, Blackhead or Coccidiosis, wash out the water containers daily with bleach water. Mix up the medicated water fresh daily. Ronidazole 20% is also a treatment for Blackhead.

The FDA has removed all injectable antibiotics from retail shelves. They are becoming available only with a Vet's Script that will need be filled at a local pharmacy. However, many online sources will allow antibiotics like Amoxicillin (Aqua-Mox) and Doxycycline (Aqua-Doxy) to be purchased in tablet form without a Vet's script. Look for them on the internet by typing Fish Antibiotics into Google. Pigeon supply sites may also offer antibiotic tablets.

The Amoxicillin (Aqua Mox) tablet dose for a 10 lb grown peacock is 500mgs once daily for 3 to 7 days or until 48 hours past the respiratory infection symptoms. The Doxycycline (Doxy Mox) tablet dose for a 10 lb grown peacock is 200mgs daily for 3 to 7 days or until 48 hours past the respiratory symptoms. The tablets can be divided into smaller doses to treat younger peacocks by weight. Metronidazole tablets can be sourced from Pigeons Supplies Plus and other pigeon supply outlets in 250 and 500mg tablets. The tablet dose for Blackhead is 500mgs daily as a single dose for 7 to 10 days or until 24 hours past the symptom of yellow poop. The treatment should be accompanied by a worm medication. Give a tablet by opening the beak and pressing it against the side. Slide it down the throat past the trachea being careful not to get it into the trachea.

If a large number of birds are being treated, these medications are available in a powdered form to medicate drinking water if sick birds are drinking normally enough to take up a therapeutic dose. The antibiotic powders can also be found at online pigeon supply sites like Pigeon

Supplies Plus and other pigeon supply sites without a Vet's Script. Follow the dosing directions on the package. Make up the medicated water fresh daily and keep it out of the sun. Wash the water containers daily with bleach water.

GAPEWORMS---gapeworms will clog up the trachea and eventually choke a bird to death. The symptoms can be gaping and coughing along with head shaking. These can also be symptoms of a respiratory infection. In the absence of a veterinarian's diagnosis, you should treat for both. Advanced stages of a Gapeworm infection may produce blood in the trachea. However, Gapeworms are uncommon in peafowl.

> TREATMENT… Ivermectin 1% injectable, Ivermectin Pour On and Moxivet Plus are very effective for Gapeworms. Apply 1cc of the Ivermectin Pour-on to the skin on the body under one wing. This might mean ripping off a few feathers first. It must be remembered that Ivermectin Pour On is not intended for internal use. It will treat worms and rid your birds of all external parasites such as lice, mites, ticks and fleas. The Ivermectin 1% can be given as a 1/2cc drench or injection under the skin. It can also be put over food. You can find it along with the Pour-on at Tractor Supply or other feed stores. Moxivet Plus is also an excellent single dose or flock worm treatment that mixes into the drinking water for a single 24 hour period. The dose is 20cc's to a gallon of drinking or 2cc's given directly as a single dose drench. Order it from Pigeon Supplies Plus or other pigeon supply sites.

MOXIVET PLUS

By: Doug Buffington

Moxivet is the very best product for deworming peafowl and ridding them of lice, mites, fleas and ticks. It has the following advantages.

1. It will treat peafowl of all ages.

2. Mixes perfectly with drinking water

3. One dose treatment with no follow up

4. Actively controls parasites for 28 days

5. Controls all worms common to peafowl

6. Kills lice, mites, ticks, fleas and internal worms

7. Expires 30 months from the date of manufacture

8. Expressly kills lice, scaly leg mites and feather mites

9. It is a single 24 hour treatment for worms, fleas, lice and mites

10. Can be given as a direct, single 2cc/ml oral dose to grown peafowl

Dosage: 20cc's/ml per gallon of drinking water. Let it stand for 24 hours only. It can also be given as a direct, single dose drench of 2ml for a grown peacock. Keep out of direct sunlight. Moxivet is a clear liquid that forms a milky white solution when mixed with water. It is not recommended for use with animals that will become a part of the food supply. An egg withdrawal has yet to be established. Rotate the use of Moxivet with Ivermectin, Levamisole or other dewormers to avoid building a resistance. Moxivet can be ordered from Pigeon Supplies Plus and other pigeon supply sites. The 250ml bottle is the best buy.

HOW TO TREAT A SICK PEACOCK

by: Doug Buffington

Typically, there are only three things that will kill Peacocks, Pheasants, and Turkeys. They are Respiratory Infections, Worms, and the Protozoans: Coccidia, Blackhead, and Canker. Metronidazole tablets in combination with the All in One medication will treat the protozoan infections plus worming them if your sick bird is drinking normally enough to take in a therapeutic dose of the medicated drinking water.

Here are the symptoms of a Protozoan Infection: Lethargy and Droopy Wings with the head pulled back. If your sick bird is breathing normally, treat it with the All in One and other medications. In more advanced cases of Coccidiosis, blood will be found in the poop from intestinal damage. Advanced cases of Blackhead can be diagnosed from the yellow bile found in the poop from liver damage.

PROTOZOAN INFECTION

If your bird is breathing normally but has stopped eating and drinking, treat protozoan infections with two 250mg or one 500mg tablet of metronidazole as a single dose given once daily for 5 to 7 days or for as long as the symptoms persist. Remember that the classic symptoms are yellow in the poop for Blackhead and red for Coccidiosis. If your peacock is drinking normally, supplement the metronidazole treatment with the All in One. Mix it at the rate of 2 tsp per gallon of water or 1/4 tsp per pint. The dose can be doubled for acutely sick birds. Only Mix up what is needed for one day's consumption and provide it fresh daily for 5 to 7 days. Repeat the All in One treatment 10 days after the end of the first one. Wash the drinking container with bleach water daily when treating for Coccidiosis, Blackhead and Canker. Keep the medicated water out of direct sunlight. If an infected bird is drinking normally and is not responding to the All in One medication or Metronidazole, Ronidazole

20% can be added to the drinking water to treat Canker and Blackhead but not Coccidiosis.

Remember, if your sick bird is not drinking normally enough, give two 250mg or one 500mg tablet of metronidazole as a single dose, once daily, as long as the symptom of yellow poop persist. But peacocks that are emaciated and pooping yellow from an acute Blackhead infection will be difficult to turn around. Metronidazole will treat Canker, Coccidiosis and Blackhead.

Open the beak and press the tablet against the side and slide it down the throat past the trachea. Be careful not to get the tablet into the trachea. Metronidazole tablets can be ordered online without a Vet's Script from Pigeon Supplies Plus or from other pigeon supply sites. It is often sold online as a fish medication under the brand names of Fix Zole, Aqua Zole and Fish Zole.

RESPIRATORY INFECTION

The symptoms of a respiratory infection will be the same as with a Protozoan Infection: Lethargy and droopy wings with the head pulled back. But a respiratory infection will also include irregular breathing. Although one of the All in One ingredients is the antibiotic Tylan, it is not enough to treat a respiratory infection. When using the All in One during a respiratory infection, give a series of two to three 2cc injections of Tylan 200 to a grown bird and 1/2 to 1cc to a bird under one year old. Go sideways into a breast or leg muscle. For those who do not believe they can give an injection, the Tylan can be syringed down the throat but it is more effectively injected into the muscle. LA 200 is also a highly effective injectable antibiotic. Give a series of three to four 3/4cc injections under the skin pinched up along the lower back of the neck closer to where the wings begin. If your sick bird is still eating normally, you can put the 3/4cc dose of LA 200 (Oxytetracycline) on a piece of bread or over some dry dog or cat food and feed it directly. It can also be given as a drench. LA 200 is sold under different brand names. One of the most common is Duramycin 72-200. Do not medicate with Oxytetracycline together with the All in One. It will conflict with the Ronidazole ingredient found in the All in One.

The FDA has removed all injectable antibiotics from retail shelves. They are becoming available only with a Vet's Script that will need be filled at a local pharmacy. However, many online sources will allow antibiotics like Amoxicillin (Aqua-Mox) and Doxycycline (Aqua-Doxy) to be purchased in tablet form without a Vet's script. Look for them on the internet by typing Fish Antibiotics into Google. Pigeon supply sites may also offer antibiotic tablets.

The Amoxicillin (Aqua Mox) tablet dose for a 10 lb grown peacock is 500mgs once daily for 3 to 7 days or until 48 hours past the respiratory infection symptoms. The Doxycycline (Doxy Mox) tablet dose for a 10 lb grown peacock is 200mgs daily for 3 to 7 days or until 48 hours past the respiratory symptoms. The tablets can be divided into smaller doses to treat younger peacocks by weight. Metronidazole tablets can be sourced from Pigeons Supplies Plus and other pigeon supply outlets in 250 and 500mg tablets. The tablet dose for Blackhead is 500mgs daily as a single dose for 7 to 10 days or until 24 hours past the symptom of yellow poop. The treatment should be accompanied by a deworming. Give a tablet by opening the beak and pressing it against the side. Slide it down the throat past the trachea being careful not to get it into the trachea.

If a large number of birds are being treated, these medications are available in a powdered form to medicate drinking water if sick birds are drinking normally enough to take up a therapeutic dose. The antibiotic powders can also be found at online pigeon supply sites like Pigeon Supplies Plus and other pigeon supply sites without a Vet's Script. Follow the dosing directions on the package. Make up the medicated water fresh daily and keep it out of the sun. Wash the water containers daily with bleach water.

WORMS

Stay current with your worming. It is important to worm sick peacocks that are suffering from Gapeworms and Blackhead. A symptom of Gapeworms is the gaping caused by the worms choking off the trachea. The Cecal worms are carrying the Blackhead protozoan that attack the liver and cause yellow bile to be present in the poop.

BLACKHEAD TREATMENT

Blackhead (Histomoniasis) is caused by an amoeba-like parasite, *Histomonas meleagridis*, that lives in the caeca of chicken, turkeys, quail, pheasants, and other gallinaceous (chicken-like) birds. The caeca are blind portions of the intestine, the equivalent to the human appendix, which is paired and large in gallinaceous birds.

Life Cycle. This is complicated! *Histomonas* is typically carried by *Heterakis* roundworms that also live in the caeca. *Histomonas* parasites are passed in Heterakis worm eggs in the droppings; the thick shell of the worm egg protects the fragile *Histomonas* organisms. If the eggs are ingested by another gallinaceous bird, the eggs hatch out in the caeca producing both more roundworms as well as allowing the *Histomonas* organism to escape and multiply and possibly cause disease.

Peacock, turkeys and quail (both native button quail (*Turnix* spp), as well as domestic quail (Coturnix spp), are typically more susceptible to Blackhead than chickens. A common scenario is that if these species are kept where they can come into contact with chicken droppings containing *Histomonas* contaminated *Heterakis* worm egg, the chickens themselves, because of their greater natural immunity, may remain well and show no signs of the disease while the other species may become very ill and die.

Great care must be taken to ensure appropriate worming if chickens are kept on the same soil as turkeys, peacocks, or quail. Preferably these species should be housed separately from chickens that are resistant carriers.

Disease *Histomonas* is especially dangerous as when it is ingested it does not remain solely in the gastrointestinal system but can migrate first to the liver and then to other organs such as the spleen, kidneys, and lungs. While migrating the parasites can cause hemorrhages and severe tissue damage resulting in high mortalities. If birds survive, extensive scarring occurs which can result in secondary complications.

Diagnosis Blackhead can be suspected in birds passing typical *Heterakis* worm eggs (identified by microscopic examination of droppings and/or a faecal flotation test) that are showing signs of illness. It needs to be differentiated from other diseases such as coccidiosis, bacterial or viral infections. A blood panel will typically show elevated liver enzymes.

Treatment consists of dosing with drugs such as metronidazole, dimetridazole or ronidazole 20%. Instructions will vary depending on which drugs are selected and manufacturer's dosage recommendations.

Note by: Doug Buffington
When a peacock is acutely infected, pooping yellow and emaciated with Blackhead, it will be very difficult to turn around. When treating for Coccidiosis, Blackhead and Canker, wash out the drinking container with bleach water daily. Mix up the medicated water fresh daily and keep it out of the sun.

TRANSPORTING PEACOCKS

Use only cotton pillowcases, cotton sacks, or burlap. Do not use plastic.

Can you Raise Chickens, Turkeys and Peafowl Together?

by: Shannon Mock

Many people will say that you cannot raise turkeys or peafowl or any game bird with chickens because of Blackhead Disease. Blackhead Disease is the common name for Histomoniasis. It is not known exactly why people call it Blackhead, because there is no blackening or darkening or any issue with infected birds' heads. The primary symptom of peafowl suffering from Blackhead is general lethargy, depression, loss of weight, or in a younger bird's general lack of weight gain and wasting. If not treated, the infected bird will eventually die.

Blackhead is caused by a protozoan, Histaminas Meleagridis, which severely damages the liver and cecum. This protozoan is usually inside the eggs/larva of a parasitic cecal worm. The eggs of the cecal worm can remain in the soil for up to three years, however, the infection does not usually occur this way. Typically, an earthworm or insect will ingest the cecal worm egg and then a bird eats this intermediate host or pecks at infected poop. The cecal worm egg and/or larva can live in an earthworm for more than a year. When birds eat an infected earthworm or insect the cecal worm larvae containing the protozoa are released.

Turkeys, peafowl, and game birds are very sensitive to these protozoa, and the protozoa thrive in the systems of these types of birds, causing much internal damage. Chickens, on the other hand, may ingest the worms and protozoa, but are rather resistant to the symptoms. The question is: Can you Raise Chickens, Turkeys and Peafowl Together?

Many people will say that you cannot raise turkeys or peafowl or any game bird and especially with chickens because of Blackhead Disease.

The problem is that chickens can carry the worms and protozoa and then spread the disease through their droppings. If you only have chickens, no one may ever know that Blackhead is present. If you have turkeys, peafowl, or game birds living with your chickens, specifically with exposure to the chickens' droppings, then the Blackhead could make your other fowl very sick. **Doug's Note:** When treating for Blackhead, Coccidiosis and Canker, wash the drinking container daily with bleach water. Make up the medicated water fresh daily and keep it out of the sun.

THREE THINGS THAT WILL KILL PEACOCKS, PHEASANTS & TURKEYS

By: Doug Buffington

Although there are about 80 different poultry diseases, basically there are only 3 things that will likely infect and kill your Peacocks, Pheasants, Turkeys and other farm birds. By themselves, each one is lethal. In combination, they are extra deadly.

All 3 LETHAL THREATS can be treated with: 5 in 1 and All in One which are both the same product sold under different names. These powders are added to water while a sick bird is still drinking normally and will control deadly protozoans like Coccidiosis and Blackhead. They will also control the four common poultry worms: large roundworms, Cecal worms, Capillary worms, and Gape worms.

If you are treating a sick bird with the 5 in 1 or All in One for a protozoan infection of Coccidiosis and Blackhead along with a respiratory infection, it is recommended that you also give a 2cc injection of Tylan 200 in the muscle of the breast or leg muscle. Give a series of 3 to 4 injections putting each in a different location. The Tylan ingredient in the All-in-One powder is not enough to treat a respiratory infection without the supplemental Tylan 200 antibiotic injections. Do not use Oxytetracycline (LA 200 & Duramycin 72-200) in combination with the All in One or 5 in 1. It conflicts with the Ronidazole ingredient of these medications.

The All in One or 5 in 1 medication must be kept on hand. They can only be ordered online from pigeon supply sites like Pigeon Supplies Plus. More acute cases will require two 250mg tablets daily from the same supply sources. Please remember, a sick bird cannot wait on the mail.

The FDA has removed all injectable antibiotics from retail shelves. They are becoming available only with a Vet's Script that will need be filled at a local pharmacy. However, many online sources will allow antibiotics like Amoxicillin (Aqua-Mox) and Doxycycline (Aqua-Doxy) to be purchased in tablet form without a Vet's script. Look for them on the internet by typing Fish Antibiotics into Google. Pigeon supply sites may also offer antibiotic tablets.

The Amoxicillin (Aqua Mox) tablet dose for a 10 lb grown peacock is 500mgs once daily for 3 to 7 days or until 48 hours past the respiratory infection symptoms. The Doxycycline (Doxy Mox) tablet dose for a 10 lb grown peacock is 200mgs daily for 3 to 7 days or until 48 hours past the respiratory symptoms. The tablets can be divided into smaller doses to treat younger peacocks by weight. Metronidazole tablets can be sourced from Pigeons Supplies Plus and other pigeon supply outlets in 250 and 500mg tablets. The tablet dose for Blackhead is 500mgs daily as a single dose for 7 to 10 days or until 24 hours past the symptom of yellow poop. The treatment should be accompanied by deworming. Give a tablet by opening the beak and pressing it against the side. Slide it down the throat past the trachea being careful not to get it into the trachea.

If a large number of birds are being treated, these medications are available in a powdered form to medicate drinking water if sick birds are drinking normally enough to take up a therapeutic dose. The antibiotic powders can also be found at online pigeon supply sites like Pigeon Supplies Plus and other pigeon supply sites without a Vet's Script. Follow the dosing directions on the package. Make up the medicated water fresh daily and keep it out of the sun. Wash the water containers daily with bleach water.

PEACOCKS, PHEASANTS AND TURKEYS are more disease prone because they are more often penned in close quarters where they tend to be chronically reinfected by worms, protozoans and bacterial disease. Also, their immune systems are not as resistant as that of a chicken.

THE 3 LETHAL PEACOCK INFECTIONS are:

- A. Respiratory
- B. Protozoan
- C. Worms

RESPIRATORY INFECTION…symptoms that include:
1. Puffy Eyes
2. Swollen Face
3. Runny Nose
4. Sneezing, Coughing, Gasping/Rasping breath

The 5 in 1 and All-in-One both contain the antibiotic Tylan but it is not enough to treat a respiratory infection. Antibiotics should be given as described above.

PROTOZOANS…are one cell parasites that will kill your birds. The symptoms are lethargy and droopy wings with the head pulled back, diarrhea and loss of weight. A classic symptom of a Coccidian and Blackhead protozoan infection is red or yellow in the poop. The 5 in 1 and All in One each contain antiprotozoals to combat protozoan infections. In more acute cases, Ronidazole 20% powder can be added to the drinking water if an infected bird is drinking normally. Please remember that Ronidazole will not treat Coccidiosis.

> The Protozoans that respond to Metronidazole and Ronidazole are: Blackhead, Hexamita and Canker. Persistent cases these protozoan will require two 250mg tablets of metronidazole daily. More acute infections will be difficult to turn around. Give a worm medication in addition to the metronidazole tablets. Cankers are white to yellow growths on the tongue, upper inside of the beak and in the throat that are spread by pigeons, doves and wild birds that eat and drink with peacocks. Canker growths can be treated with metronidazole tablets and a number of powdered medications for the drinking water. It is regrettable that these are only treatments and generally not a cure. Follow up treatments will likely be necessary. When treating for a protozoan infection, wash out the drinking containers with bleach water and make up medicated water fresh daily. Keep it out of the sun.

If a large number of birds are being treated, these medications are available in powdered form to medicate drinking water if sick birds are drinking normally enough to take up a therapeutic dose. They can be found at online pigeon supply sites like Pigeon Supplies Plus. Ronidazole 20% is a good medicated powder for mixing with drinking water to treat canker and blackhead. Canker will need 2 to 4 weeks of treatment or more. Follow up treatments may be necessary.

SYMPTOMS

1. The symptoms of blackhead and coccidiosis protozoan infections are a stooped, ruffled and lethargic peacock with droopy wings.

2. Often an infected bird will stop eating and drinking.

3. Other symptoms can be blood in the poop from intestinal damage and yellow in the poop from bile caused by liver damage.

4. Canker will cause gaping from a struggle to breath. There are medications that will treat canker but not cure it completely.

A. WORMS…are parasites that live in the bloodstream and intestines. The worms most commonly found in poultry are:
1. Roundworms
2. Capillary Worms
3. Gapeworms
4. Cecal Worms: Cecal worms damage the Cecum and carry Blackhead protozoans.

WORM TREATMENT

Worms are most often treated with Levamisole, Ivermectin 1%, Ivermectin "pour-on" and Moxivet. Give 1/4 tsp of Levamisole powder (Prohibit) to a gallon of water for 3 days mixed up fresh daily. Ivermectin 1% and Ivermectin Pour-on will not only kill all internal parasites but will also kill all external parasites such as lice, mites, ticks and fleas. Give the Ivermectin 1% as a 1/2cc drench down the throat or as a 1/2cc injection under the skin pinched up between where the wings start and the base of the neck. This is the dosage for birds over one-year-old. You can also put the Ivermectin 1% dose on a piece of bread or over some dry dog and cat food to feed it directly. Those under one year should receive a half dose or 1/4cc. The Ivermectin pour-on is a particularly good treatment for Gapeworms. Take a Q-tip and apply 1cc to the skin on the body under one wing. Expect to see relief from the gaping in 3 to 5 days. Ivermectin 1% and Ivermectin Pour-On will actively control worms and body parasites for 28 days.

No follow-up is needed for the Ivermectin pour-on or the Ivermectin 1% injection because it is effectively removing worms for 28 days. However, the All in One treatment should be followed with a recommended worm medication 10 to 12 days after the end of the treatment. Or, the All in One can be repeated. This will catch any worm eggs that have hatched after the first treatment. The All in One will also combat Blackhead and Coccidiosis. Rotate worm medications to avoid building a resistance.

Moxivet Plus is another excellent product to rotate with other worm medications. It is a single dose, 24 hour treatment mixed into drinking water. It will treat all worms common to peafowl plus flukes. No follow up treatment is required. Mix 20cc's to a gallon of water or 5cc's to a quart/liter. Moxivet can also be given as a single oral dose of 2cc's.

TO SUM IT UP…the 3 LETHAL THREATS…<u>Worms, Respiratory & Protozoans infections</u> can be treated with the 5 in 1, All in One, Metronidazole, antibiotics and Ronidazole 20%. The All in One and the 5 in 1 will also contain a combo pack of vitamins, amino acids, electrolytes and probiotics to help speed the recovery of a sick bird. Remember that the All in One and 5 in 1 do not contain enough antibiotic to treat a respiratory infection. Two, 250mg metronidazole tablets are recommended as a single dose daily when a sick bird has stopped eating and drinking or when protozoan infection symptoms are not controlled with the 5 in 1 and All in One. Canker treatments may take 10 days to two weeks. If protozoan infected birds are drinking well enough, their water can be medicated with Ronidazole 20% powder. Treat respiratory infections with injections of LA 200, 72-200 or antibiotics in tablet or powdered form.

Remember, there is evidence that using LA 200 and Duramycin 72-200 (both oxytetracycline) for a respiratory infection during an All in One or Ronidazole 20% treatment will diminish the effectiveness of the Ronidazole ingredient. It is recommended to use a different antibiotic when treating for these conditions at the same time.

POULTRY SPECIES AS BLACKHEAD RESERVOIRS

Among poultry species, there are varying degrees of susceptibility to Blackhead. Some birds, such as pheasants, ducks, and geese, are nearly immune to the effects of Blackhead. Chickens are somewhat resistant to the protozoan, while turkeys and peafowl are extremely vulnerable and have high mortality rates when infected with histomonas meleagridis (Blackhead). Experiments have shown that infected pheasants and chickens are capable of transmitting Blackhead to young turkeys and peacocks (Lund and Chute, 1972).

Traditional wisdom dictating that chickens and turkeys not be raised together is most likely based on experience with Histomoniasis (Blackhead). Chickens are excellent hosts for the cecal worm that H. meleagridis uses as a vector.

It is not unreasonable to assume that the majority of Blackhead outbreaks, especially among small, diversified farmers, can be traced back to chickens.

BLACKHEAD TRANSMISSION BY CECAL WORM EGGS & SOIL

The indirect ingestion of the Blackhead protozoa through consumption of earthworms and cecal worm eggs is a commonly known means of contracting Histomoniasis. When exposed to the elements, the Blackhead pathogen is short-lived, being highly susceptible to the environmental stresses of sunlight, wind, and temperature extremes. H. meleagridis has overcome this limitation through infecting cecal worm eggs, as these eggs are extremely hardy. The eggs can remain viable up to three years in the soil. Cecal worms are very common in many poultry species, especially chickens. Contaminated cecal worm eggs are consumed when farm birds ingest soil either intentionally or during foraging. Earthworms also act as an intermediate vehicle for spreading the disease. Earthworms consume the soil contaminated with the Blackhead protozoan which passes to peacocks and turkeys when they consume the worms. The consumption of earthworms is only one means of transmission. Birds pecking a poop and sitting on contaminated soil is another means. And, there seems to be an additional but poorly understood vector of transmission especially among crowded, commercial conditions. Some suspect the protozoans attached to dust are windblown.

BLACKHEAD TRANSMISSION BY CECAL WORM EGGS & SOIL

The indirect ingestion of Blackhead protozoa through consumption of earthworms and cecal worms are a commonly known means of contracting Histomoniasis. But often, farm birds will pick it up from pecking at fresh poop.

When exposed to the elements, the Blackhead pathogen is short-lived, being highly susceptible to environmental stresses — sunlight, wind, and temperature extremes. Histomonas meleagridids has overcome this limitation through infecting cecal worm eggs, as these eggs are extremely hardy.

The eggs can remain viable for up to three years in the soil; in addition, cecal worms are very common in many poultry species, especially chickens. Contaminated cecal worm eggs are consumed when birds ingest soil either from pecking feed from the ground or during foraging. Earthworms also act as an intermediate vehicle for spreading the disease. Earthworms consume the soil contaminated with the Blackhead protozoan which passes to farm birds when they consume the worms. It is also transmitted by the ingestion of fresh feces containing the infected ova of Heterakis gallinarum that are within earthworms.

Calcium: The Key to Beautiful Eggs and Healthy Hens

When hens begin to lay, calcium levels are important. Do you know how to make sure your hens have what it takes to make strong, unbreakable eggshells?

Calcium, like many other vital nutrients, will depend on other minerals being present. In the case of calcium, the two nutrients that affect it most are phosphorus and vitamin D3. Calcium, Vitamin D3, and phosphorus form a sort of 3-legged stool; if any of these nutrients are out of balance, the whole stool topples and problems begin.

Calcium and phosphorus
Phosphorus is a nutrient that is highly available in the cereals or grains that make up the majority of many chicken diets. However, if your birds' diet is too high in grains, phosphorus levels can cause an imbalance.

Mixing scratch and other grains into the diet of a nutritionally balanced and complete pellet/crumble can cause an imbalance of the "Cal-Phos" ratio. When phosphorus levels are too high, it will pull calcium not only from eggshell production but also from the beak, bones, and other vital areas where calcium is concentrated. Make sure that any added feeds and treats do not exceed 10% of the total diet of a balanced bagged feed.

Calcium and Vitamin D3
Vitamin D3 is also a vital partner in the absorption of calcium. While D3 is readily available in correct amounts in a balanced feed ration, its production within the body depends on sunshine which converts a D3 precursor into the form that chickens need. Making sure your flock has access to at least some sunshine all year long is important to keeping D3 levels high enough to keep calcium absorbed.

Keeping your flock on a completely balanced ration designed for laying hens is one way to keep the balance between calcium, phosphorus, and vitamin D3 correct. Feeding scratch grains will upset this balance plus it is low in protein, vitamins and especially calcium.

Doug's Note
One parting thought about grains and how they contribute to lower calcium levels. A low calcium level is a common cause of egg binding in hens. Egg binding occurs when a hen's muscles are too weak to expel the egg because the muscles lack an adequate level of calcium. When this happens, break up a Tums into 4 pieces and poke the pieces down the throat while avoiding the trachea. This will cause the egg to be laid anywhere from a few minutes to a few hours. Open the beak, press the Tums pieces against the side and slide each one down past the trachea.

FOWLPOX

Fowl Pox is transmitted by direct contact between infected and susceptible birds and by mosquitos. Virus-containing scabs around the eyes and beak can be sloughed from affected birds and serve as a source of infection. The virus can enter the bloodstream through the eye, skin wounds, or respiratory tract. Mosquitoes become infected from feeding on birds with fowl pox in their bloodstream. Mosquitos are the primary reservoir and transmitters of fowl pox on poultry ranges. Several species of mosquito can transmit fowl pox. Often mosquitoes will winter-over in commercial poultry houses so outbreaks can occur during winter and early spring. Fowl pox is a virus with no treatment. The scabs will harden and fall off in 2 or 3 weeks.

INTERNAL PARASITES OF PEACOCKS, PHEASANTS & TURKEYS

Dr. Jacquie Jacob, University of Kentucky

A parasite is an organism that lives in or on another organism (referred to as the host) and gains an advantage at the expense of that organism. The two types of internal parasites that affect poultry are worms and protozoa. Usually, low levels of infestation do not cause a problem and can be left untreated. Clinical signs of a parasite infestation include unthriftiness, poor growth, poor feed conversion, decreased egg production and death in severe cases. Also, parasites can make a flock more susceptible to diseases or worsen an existing disease condition.

ROUNDWORMS

Roundworms (nematodes) are common in poultry, waterfowl, and wild birds. Species of roundworms that affect poultry include species of large roundworms (Ascaris sp., also known as ascarids), species of small roundworms (Capillaria sp., also known as capillary worms or threadworms), and cecal worms (Heterakis gallinarum). Roundworms can cause significant damage to the organs they infest. Most roundworms affect the digestive tract; others affect the trachea (windpipe) or eyes.

Large roundworms are the most damaging of the worms common to backyard flocks. A severe infestation can cause a reduction in nutrient absorption, intestinal blockage, and death. Easily seen with the naked eye, large roundworms are about the thickness of a pencil lead and grow to 4.5 inches long. Occasionally, they migrate up a hen's reproductive tract and become included in a developing egg. The life cycle of a roundworm is direct; that is, worm eggs are passed in the droppings of infected birds and then directly to birds that consume contaminated feed, water, or feces. Also, worm eggs may be picked up by snails, slugs, earthworms, grasshoppers, beetles, cockroaches, earwigs, and other insects. Known as intermediate hosts, these insects carry the eggs and when eaten by a bird pass the eggs to the bird. Identifying and minimizing the number of intermediate hosts that poultry has contact with helps prevent the birds from being infected with worms. Several species of small roundworms can affect different parts of birds and cause a variety of symptoms. Species that infect the crop and esophagus cause thickening and inflammation of the mucous membranes located there. Turkeys and game birds are most commonly affected by such species and producers can suffer severe losses due to these parasites. Other species of small roundworms are found in the lower intestinal tract and cause inflammation, hemorrhage, and erosion of the intestinal lining. Heavy infestations result in reduced growth, reduced egg production, and reduced fertility. Severe infestations can lead to death. If present in large numbers, these worms can be seen during necropsy (examination after death). Small roundworm eggs are very small and difficult to see in bird droppings without a microscope. Medications that contain Levamisole are effective in treating small roundworms as well as other worms common to Peacocks and poultry.

CECAL WORMS

Cecal worms are commonly found in chickens, turkeys, pheasants, and peacocks. As the name implies, they grow in the ceca (two blind pouches at the junction of the small and large intestines). Although cecal worms typically do not affect chickens, the worms can carry Histomonas melegridis, a species of protozoan parasite that causes histomoniasis (blackhead) in turkeys. Turkeys, peacocks, and pheasants can contract histomoniasis by eating chicken manure containing infected cecal worm eggs or earthworms that have ingested infected cecal worm eggs. So, although chickens generally are resistant to problems caused by cecal worms, controlling the worms is still important for Peacock, Turkey and Pheasant health as well as chickens. Levamisole, Ivermectin and Moxivet are very effective in controlling cecal worms.

TAPEWORMS

Several species of tapeworms (cestodes) affect poultry. They range in size from very small (not visible to the naked eye) to more than 12 inches long. Tapeworms are made up of multiple flat sections. The sections are shed in groups of two or three days. Each section of tapeworm contains hundreds of eggs, and each tapeworm is capable of shedding millions of eggs in its lifetime. Each species of tapeworm attaches to a different section of the digestive tract. A tapeworm attaches itself by using four pairs of suckers located on its head. Most tapeworms are host-specific, with chicken tapeworms affecting only chickens, and so on. Tapeworms require an intermediate host to complete their life cycle. These intermediate hosts include ants, beetles, houseflies, slugs, snails, earthworms, and termites. For birds kept in cages, the most likely host is the housefly. For those raised on litter, intermediate hosts include termites and beetles. For free-range birds, snails and earthworms can serve as intermediate hosts. There are no approved medications for use against tapeworms, so controlling the intermediate hosts of tapeworms is vital in preventing initial infections and reducing the risk of reinfection. If you get a laboratory diagnosis of tapeworm infection, always ask which tapeworm species is causing the infection and which intermediate host is involved in the parasite's life cycle. Because the intermediate hosts for tapeworms vary greatly, it is important to identify the tapeworm species to target prevention efforts toward the correct intermediate host. Tapeworms are not a common poultry parasite.

Protozoa are single-celled organisms found in moist habitats, and they include some parasitic pathogens of humans and domestic animals. Coccidia live and reproduce in the digestive tract, where they cause tissue damage. This damage reduces nutrient and fluid absorption and causes diarrhea and blood loss. Coccidiosis (infection with or disease caused by Coccidia) can increase a bird's susceptibility to other important poultry diseases, such as necrotic enteritis. Coccidia is in nearly all poultry.

Chicks develop immunity to coccidiosis over time, with most severe cases occurring when chicks are three to six weeks old. Signs of coccidiosis include bloody diarrhea, watery diarrhea, abnormal feces, weight loss, lethargy, ruffled feathers, and other signs of poor health. Some store-bought starter feeds contain medication that controls but does not eliminate coccidia. Eating such feed allows young birds to develop resistance to the Coccidia prevalent in their environment. However, if the birds are exposed to a different species of Coccidia, they will not have immunity, and disease symptoms may result. A common medication for controlling Coccidiosis in birds not fed medicated feed is Amprolium. As mentioned above, following the instructions for administration is important for proper drug delivery and bird recovery. Vaccines are currently available that give newly hatched birds a small amount of exposure to Coccidia, allowing them to develop immunity without developing the disease.

Doug's Note: Coccidia may be the most common protozoan but there are three others that will infect Peacocks, Turkey, and Pheasants. They are Canker, Heximata, and the deadly Blackhead (histomoniasis). Outbreaks of these protozoans can be treated with the All in One and the 5 in 1 which are the same medications sold under different brand names. Additionally, these medications will treat Coccidiosis. A Blackhead infected bird can also be treated with Ronidazol 20% powder added to the drinking water if it is drinking normally. A 250mg to 500mg daily dose of Metronidazole will also treat common poultry protozoan infections when an infected bird is not responding to medicated water or has stopped eating and drinking. When treating for Canker and Blackhead, wash the drinking container daily with bleach water. Make up the medicated drinking water fresh daily and keep it out of the sun.

It is not a good practice to the house or range Peacocks, Turkeys, or Pheasants with chickens. Chickens are resistant carriers of worms, Coccidiosis, Blackhead and bacterial diseases that are easily transmitted. Remember, there is evidence that using LA 200 and Duramycin 72-200 (oxytetracycline) for a respiratory infection during an All in One or Ronidazole 20% treatment will diminish the effectiveness of the Ronidazole ingredient. It is recommended to use a different antibiotic like Tylan 200 injections or Aqua-Mox tablets when treating for these conditions with Ronidazole.

MEDICATED STARTER

By: Doug Buffington

Corid is a brand name for Amprolium. This is the medication in Starter feeds. Unlike other starters, the medicated 18% Purina Start & Grow must be fed for a full 3 to 4 months for a peacock's immune system to fully developed a resistance to Coccidiosis. What makes the medicated Purina Start & Grow different is that the synthetic growth proteins Methionine and Lysine are not cranked up to the maximum along with the protein level as other game bird and turkey starters are. If peachicks are fed a high protein turkey and game bird starter there will be a significant risk of a crippling overgrowth of the legs and toes.

If medicated starters are mixed with other feeds, the Amprolium will be diluted to a non-therapeutic level that will not control Coccidiosis. And, it is overdosing to feed a medicated starter while providing Corid (Amprolium).

The immune system of peachicks is not sufficiently developed to resist the Coccidia protozoa until they are 3 to 4 months old. It is imperative that peachicks are fed the medicated Purina Start & Grow or other medicated starters during the first 3 to 4 months that are not more than 18% to 20% protein. Also, it will not be enough to worm only the peacock in a flock. A mixed flock will need to be routinely wormed every 6 months at a minimum. Many are worming every 3 to 4 months. Chickens are more resistant carriers of protozoans that are deadly to Peacock, Pheasants, and Turkey. To be more successful with peacocks, consider phasing out chickens and guineas. They are prolific worm and germ factories.

Oral Dosing of Peafowl Medications

by: Craig Hopkins

Many peafowl medications are most effective when given orally down the throat. An oral dose of medication assures that the peafowl is getting the proper dose and that no bird has missed getting the medication. When peafowl is showing signs of illness, there is no better way to get them on the road to recovery than to give them the medication directly down their throat. While oral dosing has many advantages, it must be done properly to assure that the bird gets the full benefit of the medication and is not injured during the process. The purpose of this article is to describe and illustrate the proper method of giving an oral dose of medication to peafowl. The steps described in this article are best done with two people.

The first step in this process is to catch the peafowl and to properly restrain them so that they do not injure themselves or you. I use a large fishing net with a long retractable handle to catch the bird. The net material is not the normal coarsely woven nylon mesh. I use a tightly woven nylon mesh made especially for catching birds. Entire nets or just the mesh material can be purchased from most poultry or pheasant supply companies. Once the bird is caught, pin the bird to the ground with the net and grasp both legs firmly with a gloved hand. It is best to grasp both legs at the knee joint and to hold both legs in one hand. Remove the bird from the net and cradle it against your body so that it cannot flap its wings.

The second step is to open the bird's mouth. Your assistant should grasp the bird's top beak firmly in one hand and pry open the lower beak with the other hand. Once the mouth is open, the fingers on the upper beak can be placed between the 2 beaks to keep the mouth open.

To prevent any medication from entering the trachea, a long narrow syringe without the needle should be used to ensure that the medication is dosed down the throat past the trachea opening.

Now that the mouth is open, the bird's windpipe (trachea) needs to be located. This is the tube located at the base and top of the tongue that opens and closes as the bird breathes. Medication should not be allowed to enter the trachea as it will cause the bird to cough and even drown if too much liquid gets into the lungs. I use 3cc syringes to dose most medications. An insulin syringe works well for small doses and on young peafowl. Once the proper syringe has been selected and the proper dose of medication has been drawn into the syringe, you are ready to medicate your bird.

Open the mouth wide and insert the syringe into the mouth past the opening of the trachea and inject the medicine. For larger doses, inject the medicine slowly so that none splashes back and ends up on you or down the trachea. Once the syringe is empty, remove it from the bird's mouth and allow the bird to close its mouth. The bird can now be released.

I hope that you have found this article informative and helpful. Oral dosing of medications is a very effective method and when done properly, is completely safe for the birds and for you and your assistant. Please visit our website: www.hopkinslivestock.com to find more peafowl-related articles and photos.

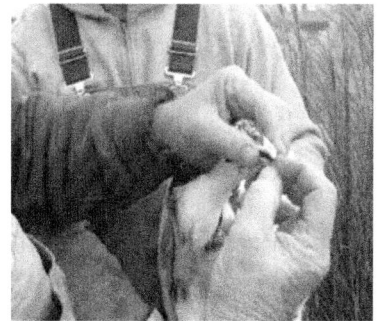

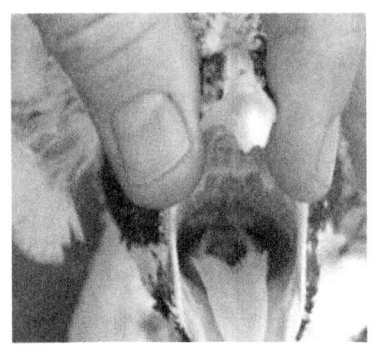 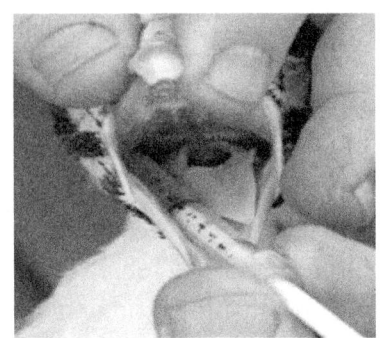

PROTOZOAN DISEASES COMMON TO PEAFOWL

A sleepy-eyed, droopy-winged bird without respiratory symptoms is most likely to have a Protozoan Infection. Below are the protozoans that infect Peacocks, Pheasants, and Turkeys.

COCCIDIOSIS

Coccidiosis is caused by a host-specific species of Eimeria and it is a protozoan common in chickens and less often in turkeys, it also occurs occasionally in geese, guineas, pigeons, pheasants, quail, and other farm birds. It is usually seen in young birds under conditions of warmth and high humidity or conditions that lead to wet litter.

The infective oocysts are present in the litter having been deposited there by infected chickens. Oocysts are easily transported by windblown dust, boots, clothing, crates, vehicle wheels, other animals, and people.

Susceptible farm birds will ingest sporulated oocysts in feed, water, litter, and become infected. If exposure is moderate, the chickens become immune to that species of coccidia. Outbreaks occur when susceptible chickens ingest massive numbers of oocysts.

Coccidia produce lesions by the destruction of epithelial cells in which they develop and multiply and by trauma to the intestinal mucosa and submucosa.

The clinical signs vary with species of coccidia. Pathogenic species cause diarrhea which may be mucoid or bloody, dehydration, ruffled feathers, anemia, listlessness, weakness, retraction of the head and neck.

HEXAMITIASIS

This is commonly found in one to nine week old turkey poults. It also occurs in gamebirds, peafowl, ducks, and pigeons. It is caused by a motile protozoan Hexamita meleagridis (Hexamita columbae in pigeons). Recovered birds often are carriers and shed the parasite in their feces which contaminate feed, water, and range. Susceptible birds get the organism by ingestion.

Initially, birds are very nervous and active. They shiver, crowd around any heat source and have subnormal temps. There is watery or foamy diarrhea and the birds dehydrate rapidly. Later on, the birds are depressed, stand with their heads retracted, feathers ruffled and wings drooping before going into coma and dying.

TRICHOMONIASIS (CANKER) This occurs in pigeons and doves and the raptors that feed on them. It is also found in turkeys, chickens, peafowl and other farm birds. Outbreaks usually occur in warm weather.

The disease is caused by Trichomonas gallinae, a motile protozoon. Pigeons are carriers and contaminate surface water or water containers. Pigeons can transmit Trichomonads to their young during feeding. Raptors expose themselves and their young by feeding them infected doves and pigeons.

The primary clinical sign in pigeons, doves, and raptors is that they have trouble closing their mouth due to oral lesions (growths). There is drooling and repeated swallowing movements with watery eyes in birds and lesions in the sinuses or periorbital area. In rare cases with penetrating cranial lesions may show central nervous system symptoms. Turkeys have a gaunt appearance with a hollowed area over the crop.

HISTOMONIASIS (BLACKHEAD)

Blackhead is caused by Histomonas Meleagidis, a protozoan that occurs most frequently in exposed, unmedicated turkeys, especially under three months. It also occurs in chickens, captive game birds and peafowl. Young farm birds are more frequently and severely affected. Their immune systems are not sufficiently developed to provide resistance until chicks are 4 months old.

It is transmitted by the ingestion of fresh feces containing the infected ova of Heterakis gallinarum that are within earthworms.

A classic symptom of Blackhead is yellow in the poop that is bile from liver damage. Initial signs are listlessness, anorexia, drooping wings, and yellow feces; the head may be cyanotic. In the later stages, there is depression, drooping wings, eyes closed, head drawn close to the body, and emaciation. The mortality may reach 100%.

PERMETHRIN 10%

Permethrin is an emulsifiable animal and premise spray with a 28-day residual effect. Kills horseflies, stable flies, lesser house flies, and other manure breeding flies, fleas, lice, mites, and ticks, including deer ticks. It will also aid in the control of cockroaches, mosquitoes, spiders, mange mites, gnats, face flies, horn flies, horseflies, ear ticks, blowflies, hog lice, poultry mites and northern fowl mites. For pests on dog premises, dilute 8oz in 6.25 gallons of water or 1 quart in 25 gallons of water…or 1.5 oz to a gallon. Spray enclosures from top to bottom and in all cracks and crevices.

For kennels, doghouses, runs, and yards, thoroughly wet pet breeding or resting areas to run off. Get it into all cracks and crevices of poultry enclosures from top to bottom. Overspray onto poultry is not toxic but **Permethrin 10% is toxic to cats. Be sure to pick up food and water before spraying.**

PROTOZOANS THAT KILL PEACOCK, PHEASANT, TURKEY & OTHER FARM BIRDS

by: Doug Buffington

Every season, a number of people panic to find lethargic birds with droopy wings accompanied by red or yellow diarrhea. These are the classic symptoms of Blackhead, Hexamitiasis and Coccidiosis. Chickens are more resistant carriers while these diseases are deadly to Peacock, Turkey, and Pheasant especially between the ages of 4 to 16 weeks. Pigeon Canker is another source of protozoan infection.

Blackhead, Hexamitiasis, Canker, and Coccidiosis are intestinal tract infections transmitted by poultry worms and fecal matter. Both the worms and the protozoans will kill the host when left untreated. In combination, they are especially deadly. Once a bird begins to show the symptoms of droopy wings and yellow or red diarrhea, it becomes challenging to save it. Because Blackhead is transmitted by Cecal worms, birds can be helped by an immediate worming in addition to medication. Every bird in the flock must be wormed in the Spring and Fall and given another round 10 days after the end of the first treatment unless a dose of Ivermectin Pour-On, Ivermectin 1% or Moxivet is used that are single treatment wormers. Peacocks ranged with chickens should be wormed every 3 to 4 months along with all other farm birds.

The All in One will go directly to control worms and to treat the protozoans that cause Blackhead, Hexamitiasis and Coccidiosis. To treat a visibly sick bird, medicate the drinking water with All in One or Ronidazole 20% for 5 to 7 days if it is drinking normally. When treating for a protozoan infection, repeat the All in One 10 days after the end of the first treatment. Mix it up fresh daily and keep it out of the sun. If a sick bird is not eating, drinking or otherwise not responding to the medicated drinking water, a treatment of metronidazole should be started. Begin a treatment with two, 250mg metronidazole tablets daily given as a single dose daily and continue the treatment as long as the symptoms persist. Open the beak and press the tablet against the side and slide it down past the trachea. Metronidazole will most often be available in 250 and 500mg tablets. Veterinarians will not always let you have the tablets so order from internet sources like Pigeon Supplies Plus and other pigeon supply sites plus Fish Antibiotic sites. When treating for Coccidiosis, Canker and Blackhead, wash the drinking container daily with bleach water. Make up the medicated drinking water fresh daily and keep it out of the sun.

It is regrettable but Metronidazole tablets, All in One and other powdered medications for drinking water are only treatments for Canker and generally not cures. Frequent follow-up treatments may be necessary. It is additionally regrettable that peacocks acutely infected with Blackhead that are emaciated and pooping yellow from liver damage will be hard to turn around. Ronidazole 20%, available at pigeon supply sites, is a good individual and flock treatment for blackheads and canker. The treatment may need to be extended for 2 to 4 weeks.

It cannot be stressed strongly enough how important it is to feed chicks a medicated starter to combat Coccidiosis. The Purina Medicated Start & Grow can be found at a Purina dealer or at Tractor Supply. Chicks are at the greatest risk for Coccidiosis for the first 3 to 4 months. Their immune systems require 3 to 4 months to fully develop. The medicated Purina Start & Grow can be fed to peacocks beyond 16 weeks. But, feeding other starters with high levels of protein above 18 to 20% will risk a crippling overgrowth in the legs and toes of the young peacocks. Additionally, if you feed high protein Game Bird Starters or Turkey Starters, they will not be medicated and you will leave your chicks without Coccidiosis protection for the 3 to 4 months it takes their immune systems to resist Coccidiosis. A higher mortality rate will result when peachicks are removed from medicated starters before 3 to 4 months of age. Please remember that a Peacock is not a release and shoot Game Bird or a Turkey being rushed to the Thanksgiving table.

Peacocks ranged with chickens or even where chickens have been for the previous three years are at a much greater risk of acquiring a protozoan infection. Chickens are more resistant, heavy shedders of Blackhead and Coccidiosis protozoans as well as worms. Those serious about keeping Peacock should consider phasing out their chickens.

Here is the Take Away:

1. Worm every March and September or every 3 to 4 months if you have Peacock ranging with chickens, guinea and other farm birds.

2. Feed the medicated Purina Start & Grow for a minimum of 3 to 4 months before moving them to the Purina Flock Raiser crumble. The flock can be fed the Purina Game Bird Layer during the laying season. Go back to the Flock Raiser crumble after the season.

3. Keep the All in One powder and metronidazole tablets on hand at all times. Give the All in One for 5 to 7 days to treat visibly sick birds. Repeat the treatment 10 days after the end of the first treatment. Keep the medicated water out of direct sunlight. If symptoms persist or your sick bird is no longer eating and drinking, give a grown bird two, 250mg metronidazole tablets as a single dose daily for as long as the symptoms persist. Peacocks, aged 3 months to one year, can be given one tablet. It is regrettable but peacocks that are acutely infected, emaciated and pooping yellow will be hard to turn around. When treating for Coccidiosis, Canker and Blackhead, wash the drinking container with bleach water. Make up the medicated drinking water fresh daily. Keep it out of the sun. Ronidazole 20% powder is a good individual or flock treatment for Canker and Blackhead if a sick bird is drinking normally. Look for it at Pigeon Supplies Plus and other pigeon supply sites. **Remember, there is evidence that using LA 200 and Duramycin 72-200 (oxytetracycline) for a respiratory infection during an All in One or Ronidazole 20% treatment will diminish the effectiveness of the Ronidazole ingredient. It is recommended to use a different antibiotic when treating for these conditions at the same time.**

WORM MEDICATIONS

by: Doug Buffington

WHEN TO WORM?

A number of breeders are asking when to worm a chick. Chicks in a coop up on wire have no way to come in contact with or otherwise be infected by worms. If a chick picks up a worm or worm egg on its first day on the ground, it will take a month before it begins to populate its system to a significant amount. So, if necessary, chicks can be wormed any time after a month on the ground.

At a minimum, peacocks should be wormed in the early Spring and again in the early Fall. Peacocks kept with chickens and other poultry should be wormed every three to four months. Do the same for Turkeys. Worm everything on the place.

We can assume that every farm bird is carrying some level of worms, coccidiosis and blackhead. When the level of these parasites gets too high it will overwhelm the ability of a bird's immune system to control them. Routine worming will keep the "worm burden" low as well as the Blackhead protozoans that are a parasite on Cecal worms. However, depending on the product, worm medications will only reduce the worm population by 92 to 98%. No wormer will expel absolutely every worm. Worms will repopulate from those left behind in the host and from what they pick up from the environment...usually from pecking at poop or feeding from the ground. A spring and fall treatment with the All in One will treat coccidiosis and blackhead in farm birds as well as expel worms. This will help your peacocks go into the laying season and the winter much healthier than without the treatment.

SAFEGUARD Many are using this wormer by mixing it with the water for 3 days. But it will settle out in the bottom of the container. Important ingredients are stuck to the bottom of the water container that are not taken in by the birds. However, if you have only a few birds to worm, you can feed one teaspoon of Safeguard on a piece of bread or drench it directly as a single treatment. Repeat the treatment in 10 days.

IVERMECTIN POUR ON The Pour on version of Ivermectin is very effective for Gapeworms. It must be remembered that it is not intended for internal use. It will treat worms and rid your birds of all external parasites such as lice, mites, fleas and ticks. For a grown peacock, apply 1cc of the Pour-On to the skin under one wing with a Q-Tip. You will need to rip a few feathers off first. Birds under six months will need one-half of the adult dosage. Because Ivermectin has a 28-day residual effect, it will not require a follow up dose.

IVERMECTIN 1% The Ivermectin 1% will control all poultry worms and external parasites like lice, ticks, mites and fleas that peafowl are likely to acquire. It can be dosed as follows: 1/2cc for a bird over one year old and 2/10cc for under six months. The dosage can be given as an injection under the skin or as a drench down the throat. Injections are given under skin pinched up at the base of the lower back of the neck closer to where the wings begin. These same dosages can be given on a piece of bread and fed directly.

For a long period of time, a dosage of 3cc per gallon of drinking water for 3 days was recommended. That recommendation has been withdrawn by many breeders because the Ivermectin 1% has very poor solubility in water. It tends to separate and float on the surface.

OXFENDAZOLE

This is a convenient and effective wormer for all of the types of worms that peafowl and other farm birds are likely to acquire. It is a powder that mixes with water and is provided fresh daily for three days. The dosage is one teaspoon per gallon of water for 3 to 4 days. Put the measured powder in a half-full bottle of warm (not hot) water and shake vigorously until thoroughly mixed. Pour it into the water container and finish filling with the recommended amount of water. Mix it up fresh daily.

LEVAMISOLE

When it is not sold simply as Levamisole, this product is sold under a number of other brand names. The most common may be Prohibit. Levamisole and its different brand names are often found available through internet sites or on Ebay. It is one of the ingredients found in the

All-in-One medication. The All in One will also treat Coccidiosis, Hexamita and Histomoniasis (Blackhead) infections. The All in One is a medication that also treats a number of worm infections. When it is used to treat worms or a protozoan infection like Coccidiosis and Blackhead, the end of the treatment should be followed 10 to 12 days later with another round of the All in One. The second treatment will catch the worm eggs that hatched since the first round. Blackhead protozoans are a parasite on the Cecal worm that need to be further reduced in number. The dosage, when only using Levamisole, is 1/4 teaspoon per gallon of water for 3 days. Mix and provide fresh daily. Keep all medicated water out of direct sunlight.

MOXIVET PLUS

Moxivet is the very best product for deworming peafowl and ridding them of lice, mites, ticks and fleas. It has the following advantages.

1. It will treat peafowl of all ages
2. Mixes perfectly with drinking water
3. Single dose treatment with no follow up
4. Actively controls parasites for 28 days straight
5. Kills lice, mites, ticks, fleas and internal worms
6. Expires 30 months from the date of manufacture
7. Expressly kills lice, scaly leg mites and feather mites
8. Can be given as a direct, single 2cc/ml oral dose to peafowl
9. It is a single 24 hour treatment for worms, fleas, lice and mites

Dosage: 20cc's/ml per gallon of drinking water. It can be given as a direct, single dose drench of 2ml for a grown peacock. Keep out of direct sunlight. Moxivet is a clear liquid that forms a milky white solution when mixed with water. It is not recommended for use with animals that will become a part of the food supply. An egg withdrawal has yet to be established. Rotate the use of Moxivet with Ivermectin, Levamisole or other dewormers to avoid building a resistance.

Moxivet can be ordered from Pigeon Supplies Plus and other pigeon supply sites. The 250ml bottle is the best buy.

When using a powdered wormer product: You may need to put the dosage in a water bottle half full of lukewarm water (not hot) and shake well. Pour it into the water container and finish filling to the desired level. Many are doing this with the Oxfendazole. It is not necessary for the Prohibit wormer or the All in One.

Alternating the wormers is a good practice to help prevent a resistance to one particular type. Remember that Safeguard and Panacur are the same product sold under different brand names. After worming your birds, you should follow the end of the treatment with another dose in 10 to 12 days to catch the eggs that have hatched since the first worming. But remember that Moxivet Plus and Ivermectin are single dose treatments without a follow up.

NO CHICKS IN THE BATHTUB PLEASE

by: Doug Buffington

Please take your peachicks out of the bathtub, the washtub, shower stall, water tank, pet carrier, fish aquarium and birdcage. These are not spaces to hold a chick until it is big enough to throw out the back door to "free-range" the neighborhood.

Every year there are breeders with 2 to 4-week-old chicks gasping for air. All of them have been kept as described above or outside on the ground in a horse stall, bird cages or other area without the benefit of a heat lamp and proper bedding. Eventually they will be asking why are they having trouble breathing.

Peachicks should not be kept inside or outside without a heat lamp. Many are keeping chicks under the AC as well. Gasping chicks with respiratory issues are just about impossible to turn around. Some, "because it is too hot outside," will bring the chicks inside under the AC and put them back out at night. Those are two different climate zones. A chick should not be exposed to either of them without caution…let alone twice daily. A great number of chicks kept inside will eventually get sick, die or suffer poor leg development in a cramped cage.

Wonky legs are caused by chicks that have outgrown their small indoor enclosure and have not received adequate exercise. Exercise is necessary for proper leg development. As a chick gains weight without exercise the legs, tendons, toes and joints will begin to give irreversible problems.

When "house chicks" end up laying on their side and gasping for air, they have acquired a respiratory infection and will die. Chicks are just about impossible to turn around when they get to this point.

To raise peacocks or any other type of farm bird you will need a proper brooder, a 8x3x3' coop under a shelter. From there, a pen or a well-fenced, spacious poultry yard with a shelter to release them to after 3 to 4 months or older. The fence needs to be a minimum of 5 feet tall. An outside dog will also help keep predators out.

BLACKHEAD, COCCIDIOSIS, CANKER TREATMENT WITH METRONIDAZOLE

(WHEN YOU HAVE A SICK BIRD THAT IS NO LONGER EATING OR DRINKING)

By: Doug Buffington

Vinegar, herbs, Cayenne pepper, Oregano and other kitchen spices will not help with Blackhead and Coccidiosis or worms. Only Metronidazole tablets will save any type of poultry from these when it is no longer eating or drinking. Metronidazole can be given as a single daily dose of two, 250mg tablets for as long as the symptoms persist. Ten days may enough but acutely infected peafowl that are emaciated and pooping yellow from liver damage will be hard to turn around.

There are a number of things you can do to immensely diminish the incidence of Blackhead and Coccidiosis among your peacocks.

First, raise the peachicks for 3 to 4 months in a wire-bottomed coop off the ground. The immune system of a peacock does not develop its full resistance to Coccidiosis and Blackhead until it is 3 to 4 months old. Feed a medicated starer of not more than 20% protein during the 3 to 4 months.

Second, consider phasing out the chickens. They are worm and germ factories. Chickens are resistant carriers of Coccidiosis, Blackhead, and worms. The Blackhead protozoan is a parasite to the Cecal worm which in turn is a parasite to peacocks. Regular worming of peacocks will help keep down the incidence of Blackhead by reducing the Cecal worm "burden." At a minimum, worm peacocks in the early Spring and again in the early Fall. Many are worming every 3 to 4 months when peacocks are penned or kept in proximity to chickens.

Third, keep 250mg tablets of metronidazole on hand. Vets are not likely to dispense metronidazole without bringing a sick peacock to the office. But Metronidazole can often be ordered from pigeon supply sites and Fish Antibiotic sites without a Vet's script.

If you talk to a Vet, explain that it is not for an animal that is part of the food supply. If needed, remind the Vet that Metronidazole leaves a bird's system in less than 48 hours.

The classic symptom of Blackhead is a lethargic peacock with droopy wings with yellow in its poop. This is bile from the liver damage that the Blackhead protozoan is causing. The symptoms for Coccidiosis are a lethargic, droopy-winged peacock with red in the poop which is blood from intestinal damage. Canker will show as a whitish to yellowish growth in the beak, throat and tongue. It will eventually choke a peacock or other farm bird. Canker is not common among peacocks unless pigeons or doves share their feeding and watering sources. Give two, 250mg tablets as a single dose daily for as long as the symptoms persist. Ten to fourteen days is usually enough. More acute cases may take longer. Begin the treatment as soon as you observe the symptoms. Delaying the treatment will impair the progress of a recovery. Open the beak and press the table against the side. Slide it down past the trachea being careful not to get it into the trachea. Ronidazole 20% powder is a good individual and flock treatment if infected birds are drinking normally. It is regrettable but the medications are only treatments for Canker infected birds and generally not a complete cure. Follow up treatments for Canker may be necessary. Segregate any peacocks being treated for Blackhead, Canker and Coccidiosis. Wash out the water containers with bleach water daily.

ALL - IN - ONE POWDER

Ingredients: Ronidazole, Amprolium, Levasole, Tylosine (Tylan)

VITA-PRO COMBO PACK OF: Electrolytes... Amino Acids...Vitamins...Probiotics

Available at Pigeon Supplies Plus and other pigeon supply sites

PARASITES & SYMPTOMS CONTROLLED BY "ALL IN 1"

1. ROUNDWORMS… droopiness, weight loss, diarrhea
2. CAPILLARY WORMS… droopiness, weight loss
3. CECAL WORMS..unthrifty, weakness, weight loss
4. GAPEWORMS... worms in the trachea, yawning, gasping, gaping

PROTOZOAN INFECTIONS TREATED BY "ALL - IN - ONE"

1. BLACKHEAD (look for droopy wings and yellow in the poop)
2. COCCIDIOSIS (look for droopy wings and red in the poop)
3. HEXAMITA (lethargic and droopy wings)
4. CANKER (repeated opening and closing of beak, gasping for air)

TYLAN POWDER
Although the All in One has Tylan Powder as one of its ingredients, it will not be enough to treat a respiratory infection.

ALL in ONE DOSAGE: 2 tsp per gallon for 5 to 7 days. The dose can be doubled when treating acutely sick birds that are drinking normally. Mix the medicated water up fresh daily. Your sick bird must be drinking normally to take up enough of the medicated water to be therapeutic. If your bird is not drinking normally, treat protozoan infections with two 250mg tablets of Metronidazole tablet daily for 5 to 7 days or for as long as the symptoms of red or yellow in the poop persist. Ask your Vet for the tablets or order them online from Pigeon Supplies Plus or other pigeon supply sites. Repeat the All in One 10 days after the end of the first treatment. Remember that the All in One should not be used for routine worming to avoid building a resistance. When medicating drinking water, only mix up the amount needed for one day's consumption and provide it fresh daily. Keep it out of the sun. And, wash out the drinking containers with bleach water daily.

It is regrettable that the All in One, along with a number of other Canker medications, are only treatments and often not complete cures. Peacocks are infected by pigeons and doves that eat and drink with them. Segregate all infected peacocks. The symptoms are a gapping breath and white to yellow growths in the throat, on the tongue and upper inside of the beak. Frequent follow up treatments may be necessary.

Rember, there is evidence that using LA 200 and Duramycin 72-200 (oxytetracycline) for a respiratory infection during an All in One or Ronidazole 20% treatment will diminish the effectiveness of the Ronidazole ingredient. It is recommended to use a different antibiotic when treating for these conditions.

THE TRUTH ABOUT FEEDING PEACOCKS, PHEASANTS & TURKEYS

by: Doug Buffington

There is no perfect feed for peacocks, pheasants and turkeys. The bagged feeds at the feed mills are formulated for chickens, turkeys, and pheasant that are not expected to live more than a few months to a couple of years. The game bird feeds are often for release and shoot pheasant farms who want to rush their chicks out before the guns in the shortest time possible. Turkeys are rushed from 3 ounces to 12 pounds in only a few months. Chickens go into Campbell's soup cans as soon as their egg production begins to fall below their peak. Then there are those chickens that are not expected to make it to egg-laying. So, we need to find a compromise among the different bagged feeds available just like we do for the poultry and livestock medications we use. It does not help to add a gob of this and a scoop that to a bagged feed with the hope that somehow it is being enriched when, in fact, it is being degraded. But it seems that everybody has a secret home blend formula.

The Purina recommendation is to use the medicated Purina Start & Grow for chicks for a minimum of 4 months before moving to a Flock Raiser crumble. Feed the Purina Game Bird Layer crumble during the laying season beginning a month before the first egg is expected. After the season, return to feeding the Flock Raiser crumble. This is a good feeding regimen. These feeds can be found at Tractor Supply or at any Purina dealer. They are very well suited to feed to peafowl.

Everything You Need to Know About Wry Neck

by: Kendill Fox, Freedom Ranger Hatchery

The health of your Peacocks should be at the top of your priority list. Without a healthy flock, egg production will be lower, sickness can spread and peacocks will die. There are certain conditions, like wryneck, that can be very alarming. At Freedom Ranger Hatchery, we want to alleviate some of those fears by sharing our years of experience.

What is Wry Neck?

Wryneck— sometimes called "crookneck," "twisted neck," or "stargazing"—is a condition that typically affects newborn chicks, and sometimes even full-grown farm birds. If you notice that your bird has difficulty standing, that its neck twists, or it seems like it is permanently looking upwards, they likely have developed a wry neck.

Typically, this condition can be caused by a genetic disorder, a vitamin deficiency, a head injury, or from ingesting toxins. Regardless of how your bird developed a wry neck, it is likely that the affected chick will not be able to hold its head up on its own. This will cause it to fall over or lie on its back, have difficulty eating, and may lead to the bird's death.

Can a Chick Live with Wry Neck?

Yes, your chick can live with a wry neck. Seeing one or more of your birds with neck twists can be difficult. It is stressful not only for the bird but likely for you as well to see your animal in such distress. The good news is that it is a curable symptom given time and patience.

The main reason why chicks die after they develop a wry neck is that they are unable to eat or drink properly. In addition, they also may not be able to move well and get trampled or pecked by other chicks.

How to Treat Wry Neck

In order to properly treat wrynecks, you first need to separate the affected bird from the rest of the flock. This condition is not contagious, but as mentioned earlier, other birds may trample or peck a disabled chick. Keeping your bird separated will also help keep its stress levels down.

Second, you'll need to up the bird's vitamin intake, specifically vitamin E and selenium (to help all the vitamins absorb more effectively). Vitamins should be administered two to three times a day until the bird's symptoms improve. There are various vitamin supplements available that contain both of these.

During this healing time for your chick, you will likely need to help the affected chick eat and drink because its neck twist will make movement difficult. Helping your chick's wry neck is a bit of a time-consuming process, but overall will make for a happier and healthier bird.

Doug's Note: Vitamin E with Selenium paste can be purchased in a syringe from Tractor Supply. Put the paste into the beak 2 or 3 times daily until the neck straightens out. Do not delay the beginning the treatment.

How Long Does it Take for Wry Neck to Go Away?

Unfortunately, the wry neck does not go away quickly. It takes time, patience, and a gentle hand to help your chick through this difficult and stressful time. Once you start administering a vitamin E and selenium supplement, you may see improvement in as little as 24 hours, but you are not out of the woods yet.

Over the following few days, your chick's symptoms may fluctuate a lot and sometimes get worse before they get better. Keep giving your chick the vitamin E and selenium and be patient—it can take up to a month before the condition completely dissipates.

How Can I Prevent Wry Neck?

By now you understand that a wry neck is caused mostly by a deficiency in vitamins, so it's important that your birds are constantly fed a proper, nutritious diet. Like most health issues, it is easier to prevent neck twists in your birds than it is to heal them. If you are seeing crook necks in your chicks, the breeder birds are likely not receiving enough vitamin E.

Doug's Note: Tractor Supply has the Lamb and Kid Selenium/Vitamin E Gel that is very effective in treating Wry Neck. Put some in the beak twice daily or feed directly on a piece of bread if possible.

What You Need to Know about MG & MS

(Freedom Ranger Hatchery)

MG (Mycoplasma gallisepticum) and MS (Mycoplasma synoviae) are both common bacterial infections that affect chickens, turkeys, peafowl, and other avian species. Found most often in backyard flocks or multi-age commercial layer operations, MG and MS can result in severe economic losses due to slow growth rates in broilers or diminished egg production in layers.

MG, also known as chronic respiratory disease (CRD) attacks the respiratory system of infected birds and can weaken their immune systems, making them more susceptible to other infections. MS can also affect the respiratory system of infected birds, but another form of the disease attacks the joints.

Signs of Infection

Chickens infected with MG may show no signs of infection, especially if there is no accompanying secondary infection. Common signs of infection include sticky discharge from the nostrils, foamy discharge from the eyes, and swollen sinuses. Often the air sacs in the lungs become infected, resulting in rattling sounds and sneezing. Affected chickens may fail to grow and gain weight or have poor egg production.

Peafowl that are infected with MS that affects the joints will develop lameness which is followed by a reluctance to move, swollen joints, stilted gait, weight loss, and general lethargy. Those infected with the respiratory form of MS show signs of respiratory distress, similar to infection with MG. It is often not possible to distinguish between MS and MG without administering a blood test.

Transmission

Both MG and MS are fragile organisms that cannot survive more than a few days without a host, but these diseases can be spread to offspring through eggs or through natural breeding with an infected mate. Sick or recovering birds can also spread infections through nasal or eye discharge or fecal matter to other birds in the flock. Once infected, chickens are carriers of these diseases for life, though they may not show symptoms until they are stressed. MG and MS can also be carried by humans when egg flats, cages, coops, tools, equipment, or clothing have been contaminated with respiratory secretions or droppings from infected birds. Wild birds or rodents can also carry the infection and spread it to the flock.

MG & MS Prevention

Start with Disease-Free Birds

The best way to control MG and MS is to begin your flock with disease-free birds, then practice scrupulous biosecurity to protect your flock. Chicks should always be purchased from MG or MS-free flocks. Care must be taken to avoid purchasing adult birds with unknown MG or MS status.

Minimize Contact with Other Flocks

Be sure to change your clothing and footwear if you have visited other birds before coming in contact with your own flock. Also be sure to thoroughly clean and disinfect tools and equipment when they have been used in other areas of the farm or in the vicinity of other flocks. You may also want to use a set of dedicated tools and equipment for each flock to avoid contamination.

Keep Rodents & Wild Birds Away

Begin a pest control plan to keep rodents and wild birds away from your flock. Both rodents and wild birds can carry the disease and infect your birds.

Boost Immunity with the Right Diet

Never feed scratch grains. They are very nutrition poor and promote egg binding due to a lack of calcium. Begin by feeding the medicated Purina Start & Grow for the first 4 to 5 months. Then switch to the Purina Flock Raiser crumbles. The Purina Game Bird Layer is especially good for peafowl during the laying season. After the season, go back to the Flock Raiser. Purina feeds can be found at Tractor Supply or at any Purina dealer.

Quarantine New Birds

Be sure to quarantine any new members of the flock at least 12 yards away for a minimum of 4 weeks in order to avoid infecting your flock.

MG & MS Treatment

While antibiotics can be used to treat infected birds and eliminate clinical symptoms, treated birds will still be carriers of either MG or MS. The most common antibiotics for treatment include Tylan 200, Baytril and LA 200.

In order to completely eliminate MG or MS, it is necessary to harvest or cull infected broilers. Layers are often eliminated at the end of their laying cycle. Complete disinfection, followed by a rest period is recommended before establishing a new flock.

While both MG and MS are not usually life-threatening to your flock, these infectious diseases can limit the productivity of your flock, and result in losses from slow growth and poor egg production. That is why it is so important to start your flock with healthy birds, practice solid biosecurity, and always quarantine new additions appropriately to avoid infecting your flock.

What is Aspergillosis

How to Prevent It

(Freedom Ranger Hatchery)

Aspergillosis is a non-contagious respiratory disease caused by a fungal species known as Aspergillus. Commonly referred to as mycotic pneumonia, brooder pneumonia, or fungal pneumonia, Aspergillosis affects chickens, ducks, turkeys, waterfowl, game birds, peacocks, and many other bird species.

Young birds are the most susceptible to infection, though older birds under stress or with compromised immune systems can develop chronic Aspergillosis.

Infection with Aspergillosis occurs through the inhalation of spores, typically from contaminated litter or other contaminations. Infection in young chicks is usually the result of inhaled spores from a contaminated incubator when the infected eggs hatch and release large numbers of spores which are inhaled by other chicks.

The incidence and severity of the disease increase under warm, wet, or humid conditions. Dusty conditions and environments that result in high levels of ammonia are also perfect breeding grounds for Aspergillosis. That is why contaminated poultry bedding is one of the most common sources of infection.

Signs and Symptoms

Aspergillosis mainly affects the respiratory system of infected birds, invading the trachea, air sacs, and lungs. An infection is typically described as acute or chronic.

Acute infections typically occur in young chicks. Symptoms develop in the first 3-5 days after exposure. The most common symptom is rapid, open-mouthed breathing (gasping) due to gradual air passage obstruction.

As the disease progresses, young chicks will eventually exhibit a lack of appetite, emaciation, increased thirst, and drowsiness. Eye swelling, blindness, and torticollis (twisting of the neck to one side) are also typical of Aspergillosis infections.

Chronic forms of Aspergillosis usually affect older birds or birds with compromised immune systems. Chronic infections can lead to severe respiratory distress, eye discharge, blindness, and neurological dysfunction.

How It Is Spread

Aspergillosis in birds is not contagious from bird to bird. Birds are typically infected by inhaling spores found in the environment through moldy litter, poor quality feed, and poor bedding management practices. Factors that promote infection of Aspergillosis include:

- Warm, wet environments
- Poorly ventilated areas
- High humidity environments
- Long-term feed storage
- Impaired immunity

Treatment of Aspergillosis

There is no known treatment for Aspergillosis in infected birds, so prevention is key to controlling the disease and protecting flocks.

Aspergillosis Prevention

In order to effectively prevent Aspergillosis infection in your flock, it is important to control the factors that can lead to the growth of Aspergillosis spores.

Practice Good Sanitation

Poor chicken house sanitation leads to food and bedding contamination and promotes the growth of fungus. Be sure to clean and disinfect equipment and air ducts in hatchery and brooder areas regularly. Thoroughly clean feed and water utensils regularly to avoid cross-contamination of feed or bedding supplies. Frequently relocate feeders and water dispensers to discourage mold build-up.

Safeguard Feed Supplies

Store feed in clean, dry containers to avoid contamination with mold spores. Discard uneaten food to avoid fungal growth. Avoid dusty feeds that can spread fungal spores throughout the environment.

Safeguard Bedding

Replace bedding regularly to discourage the growth of fungus. Discard wet bedding as soon as possible.

Egg Handling

Store eggs destined for hatching away from dusty areas that may contain spores. Handle, transport, and store eggs to avoid sweating, which creates moisture that promotes fungal growth.

It is clear that Aspergillosis is a deadly disease that can adversely affect the productivity of your flock and result in financial losses. The good news is that there are steps you can take to protect your chicks and minimize exposure to Aspergillosis infections. Practicing good sanitation, safeguarding feed, regularly replacing bedding, and handling and transporting eggs properly are the keys to a healthy, happy flock.

GENERAL CARE OF PEACOCKS

by: Craig Hopkins

Peafowl are native to India, Burma, Java, Ceylon, Malaya, and Congo. Peafowl are relatives to pheasants. The main difference between peafowl and pheasants is in the plumage. Peafowl are very hardy birds and with proper care, can live forty to fifty years. The term "peafowl" refers to the species name. The male is called the peacock and the female is called the peahen. Offspring under the age of one year are called peachicks.
Peafowl come in a wide variety of colors including blue, green, white, light brown, and purple. These colors and many other colors which were not mentioned have come from selective breeding done by people all over the world. The India blue and the green peafowl are the two most common colors of peafowl found in the wild. India blue peafowl are by far the most common peafowl in captivity and they are what most people are familiar with from visits to zoos and parks.

BREEDING

Peafowl normally reach the breeding age at two years. Peahens will sometimes lay fertile eggs as yearlings. They will lay these eggs late in the summer after they have turned one year old. The best chance for a yearling hen to lay eggs is when she is in the same pen as a mature male. A mature male is a peacock that is at least three years old. A peacock will not have a full tail train until he is three years old. The tail train will lengthen and get fuller over the next two to three years. After the peacock is five or six years old, the tail train will remain consistent in length and quality for the rest of the bird's life as long as the bird remains healthy. The tail train is very important to the breeding cycle of peafowl. The peacock will molt the tail in late summer and this is when the breeding season will end. A two-year-old peacock that has a one to two-foot-long tail train will be a better breeder at this age than a peacock of the same age that do not have a tail train of any size.

A mature peacock in prime condition can be mated to as many as five peahens. The egg fertility rate for each male should be monitored closely to determine how many peahens each male is capable of mating with successfully. When selecting peafowl for breeding purposes, unrelated males and females should be selected. Inbreeding can lead to many problems with both the eggs and the chicks. No matter what age peafowl are purchased or raised for breeding purposes, the birds must be healthy. A healthy bird will be active, have good feather quality, straight legs and toes, and clear eyes.

Peahens begin laying eggs in April and will lay eggs every other day until a clutch of seven to ten eggs is achieved. The eggs are light brown in color and are similar in size to turkey eggs. If the eggs are collected from the nest for artificial incubation, a peahen may lay as many as thirty eggs. Peahens, which are allowed to roam freely about a farm, will hide their nests in tall grass, around shrubs, and in brush piles. The nest is a depression scratched out in the ground and lined with grass. Nests in such locations are many times destroyed by possums, raccoons, and skunks which will eat the eggs. Peahens that are sitting on these nests are vulnerable to attack by coyotes, fox, and stray dogs which will kill the peahen. Peahens which are kept in flight pens will use old tires, wooden nest boxes, and empty barrels for nest sites. They should be filled with hay or straw to provide nesting material.

INCUBATION

There are several methods of incubating peafowl eggs. The first method is artificial incubation. Eggs are incubated at 99-100 degrees F and at a wet-bulb temperature of 86 to 87 degrees Fahrenheit. The eggs will hatch after 27 to 30 days of incubation. The eggs should be candled after 10 days of incubation to check for fertility. If an egg is not fertile, it should be removed from the incubator so that it does not spoil and possibly contaminate other eggs in the incubator. Eggs should be placed in the incubator as soon as possible after they are laid and no eggs should be held more than 10 days before incubation begins. This rule also applies to the alternative incubation methods that will be covered next.

Natural incubation of peafowl eggs can be done in several ways. The first is to allow the peahen to set on her own eggs and hatch them herself.

Peahens normally do a good job of incubation but this method limits the number of eggs that a peahen will produce for the year. Once she is sitting on a clutch of eggs, she won't lay any more eggs for that season. Occasionally, if a nest is destroyed during incubation, a peahen will lay a second clutch of eggs and set on them. The second method of natural incubation, which allows for maximum egg production, is the use of broody chickens or ducks. The peafowl eggs are collected as they are laid and then set as a clutch under a chicken or duck. The size of the clutch is determined by the size of the chicken or duck to be used for incubation. The eggs are left under the foster parent until two days before the normal hatch date. The eggs are removed from the nest and put in a hatcher. A new clutch of eggs is put under the hen and the process is repeated. If the eggs are allowed to hatch under the foster hen, the risk of disease in the chicks is much greater, and many times the hen will not stay broody to allow for more eggs to be set under her.

BROODING

The rule of thumb in brooding peafowl chicks is to start the chicks out with a brooder temperature of 95 degrees Fahrenheit and decrease this temperature by 5 degrees for every week of age. Brooders can be made at home or can be bought commercially. The brooder should provide a consistent heat source so that the chicks do not become chilled or overheated. The heating area should be large enough so that the chicks do not have to pile on top of one another to stay warm. The brooder should have a wire bottom floor so that droppings and wasted feed fall through. Brooders with feed and water troughs attached to the outside help keep the chicks healthy because the chicks cannot get into them and make a mess out of the feed and water. The last thing that a brooder must have is a lid. Chicks that are only a few weeks old are surprisingly good flyers.

The chicks are usually left in the hatcher for a day after they hatch. This gives them plenty of time to completely dry off and to gain enough strength to stand. If you have a cabinet incubator, you can leave them in the hatching tray for the first three days. Typically, chicks do not need to eat or drink during the first three days while they are feeding on the yolk. The chicks are then placed in a small wooden brooder using a heat lamp for warmth. Chicks under a week old should be kept in small groups so that they learn to eat and drink without having to compete with one another. Chicks sometimes need to be taught to eat and drink. This can be done by placing a teacher chick, which is 3 to 4 days older and has learned to eat and drink, in with the new chicks. Baby chickens or pheasants can also be used as teacher chicks. If no teacher chick is available, I place a shiny marble in the feed and water container for the chicks to pick at. While picking at the marble, they will learn to eat and drink at the same time. I also provide the chicks with finely chopped lettuce along with their starter feed. The green color of these seems to attract the chicks' attention and provides a natural food source for the chicks.

FEEDING

Peafowl are not finicky in what they eat. They will eat shelled corn, cracked corn, oats, rabbit pellets, dog food, trout chow, sunflower seed, grass, dandelions, insects, and many other foods. Because peafowl are members of the pheasant family, their diet should be structured with this in mind rather than feeding them like a chicken. Breeders are fed a Flock Raiser during the months prior to and after the breeding season. Peachicks are fed a medicated starter feed for the first three to four months minimum. After four months old, the chicks are fed Flock Raiser until they reach breeding age. However, in a mixed flock, the chicks can be fed the Purina Game Bird Layer right along with the breeders. Current year hatches will be over six months old by the time laying season begins and the remainder of the flock is feeding on the Layer ration.

HOUSING

The housing requirements for peafowl are dictated by the age of the birds. As mentioned earlier, chicks can be kept in small brooders until they reach the age of three months when they no longer require heat unless they are late hatches going into the winter. The chicks can then be kept in small buildings or a large flight pen until they are sold or reach breeding age. Breeders require much more room because of the males' long train. A flight pen for breeders should be at least six feet tall and ten feet wide so that the male can fully spread his tail. The length of this flight pen should be determined by the number of birds to be kept in this pen. For example, a pen for a trio of breeders should be twenty feet long with a building or shelter attached to the end. The flight pen must be covered with wire or netting because peafowl are strong fliers. The building or shelter should be six feet tall and be at least eight feet wide and eight feet long. The roosts should be placed four to five feet off the ground and made so that they can be removed if a hen starts laying eggs while up on the roost. A flat roost such as a 2" X 4" should be used rather than a round roost. If a round roost is used, there is a chance that the birds' toes will suffer frostbite in extremely cold weather because the toes are exposed while gripping the roost. A flat roost allows the bird to sit on its feet without having to grip the roost which prevents frostbite from occurring.

MISCELLANEOUS

Peafowl are very hardy birds but there are a few preventive steps that can be taken to ensure the health of the birds. The easiest way to keep adult peafowl healthy is to worm them at least twice a year. Many of the diseases that peafowl are susceptible to are being carried by internal parasites. There are several wormers available that can be given orally or mixed in the drinking water. The use of wire-bottomed cages and brooders will help keep the chicks healthy. Feeding a medicated starter to the chicks will help prevent coccidiosis. The starter feed should be kept fresh because these medications lose their effectiveness over time. Chicks can also be given medication in their drinking water for various other diseases.

Peafowl are one of the most beautiful birds in the world. The selective breeding of these birds has provided colors that mother nature had never even imagined. Raising peafowl has been a hobby of mine for many years and I continue to learn new things about these birds every day.

This article was written as a source of information for people who are interested in raising peafowl or for people who already own peafowl but enjoy reading about different ideas on how to raise these beautiful birds.

Nesting Boxes for Peafowl

by: Craig Hopkins

Peahens nest on the ground in the wild. They will scrape out a shallow depression in the ground and line it with grass or whatever vegetation is available. The nest is concealed underbrush, in high grass, along a fence row and etc. I would like to share with you a couple of nest box designs that I use after observing the habits of our free-range peafowl on our farm here in Indiana. I have seen our peahens use a second-story hay and straw maw many times to hide their nests. I had one peahen make a nest twice on top of lumber stored about 10' in the air above one of our tractors stored inside our tool shed. This peahen laid her eggs on top of the boards which turned out to be a poor choice since a couple would always roll away from the nest and fall to the floor. This is how I found her nest both times when the broken eggs were discovered. After observing this behavior many times, I started providing nest boxes for my peafowl using the designs that I will describe in the following paragraphs.

The first nest box design is a triangular-shaped nesting platform made of wood. I use rough sawn 1" x 6" lumber to make this platform. The sides of the platform are 32" long. The front of the platform is 46" long. The boards that form the bottom of the platform extend beyond the sideboards by 6" on each side of the platform. This is done so that the entire platform can be secured in a corner of the shelter. Once the platform is constructed and secured in a corner, hay or straw is used to line the platform to create the nest. Peahens will not carry nesting material up to the nesting platform on their own. I add a porcelain goose egg to act as a fake nest egg to encourage the hens to use the nest.

The second nest box design is one that uses an empty plastic 55-gallon drum that has been rinsed out thoroughly. Using a jigsaw or reciprocating saw, cut the drum in equal thirds. Keep the top and bottom sections and discard the middle ring. Attach a couple of 2"x 4"s to the top and bottom sections of the drum so that they can be secured in a corner of the shelter. Hay or straw and a fake nest egg are added to complete the nest boxes.

I mount these nest boxes about 5' above the floor of the shelter. The height is not critical. Mount them so that egg collection is easy. I collect my eggs daily so that the peahens do not start to sit on the nest. Multiple hens will use these nest boxes and it makes it very easy to collect eggs since they are in one location. These nest boxes keep the eggs clean and safe. Both of these nest boxes can be used on the ground as well. I would suggest adding some weight to the bottom of the plastic drum nest boxes so that they do not tip over easily.

I have found both of these designs to be very effective and they last forever if they are mounted inside of the peafowl shelters. I hope that you have found this article helpful and thank you for reading it. I have learned through many years of raising birds and animals that many of the best ideas come from observing how mother nature does things.

Peafowl Flight Pen Construction

By: Craig Hopkins

Planning and building the pens for peafowl is one of the most important tasks that peafowl breeders will face as their flock size grows. The pens should provide plenty of space for the peafowl to breed and to coexist without being overcrowded. Pens should provide security from both airborne and ground-based predators. Properly designed pens can keep peafowl healthy by preventing feral birds from entering the pens and transmitting diseases to the peafowl. Feral birds can also eat a lot of peafowl feed when flocks descend on poorly designed pens.

Injuries to peafowl and their owners can be avoided by designing the pens so that the peafowl can be sorted and relocated without having to catch the birds in a net or cage. The purpose of this article is to share many of the ideas that we have incorporated into our twelve, new flight pens. Please see the enclosed drawing of our flight pens to find the dimensions and details of our design work.

I have raised animals and birds all my life and these experiences have helped me to design our flight pens to allow for easy handling and sorting of birds without having to catch them. If you have ever attended a livestock auction in person you will have seen that the animals are moved by a series of gates and aisleways. We have incorporated this idea into our flight pens by making an 8' wide aisle that runs the entire width of our flight pens. The end gate of each flight pen opens into this aisle way and will swing open a full 90 degrees. This allows for birds to be driven into the aisle way for sorting or moving to a new pen without being caught. The aisle way also serves as a security feature as well by providing a second enclosure that the birds would have to escape from in order to get away into the wild. This idea is taken from zoos that have large aviaries for birds that humans can enter and interact with the birds. There are always 2 doors or gates that the people have to go through in order to enter or exit the aviary. Gates are positioned at each end of the aisle way and in the middle to provide maximum access for grass mowing, landscaping equipment and etc. The aisle way gates swing out so that if a bird were to ever escape, they could be driven back into the aisle way with ease as long as they were on the ground. Small swinging gates are used in each pen to allow us to access each pen without having to walk through the entire length of each pen or having to walk through the box stalls. These gates can also be used to move birds from pen to pen.

The wooden structure of our pens is built on standard 8' on-center construction. This method was chosen so that the pens match up identically in width to the heated box stalls on the inside of our pole barn. The box stalls are 8' wide, 8' deep, and 8' high. The outside, flight pens are 8' wide, 42' long, and on average, 8' high.

We will keep pairs or trios of our breeder peafowl in each pen. Our pens are built on the south side of our pole barn to provide maximum shelter from the cold, northwest, winter, winds and to take advantage of any winter sunshine. The first 10' of the pens, leading away from the pole barn, are covered with metal, siding that matches our pole barn. This provides a covered resting area for the birds and provides protection to the box stall entry doors from wind, rain, and snow. All of the lumber used in our flight pens is pressure treated by a new process called Micronized Copper Quaternary (MCQ). The advantages of this new process are that the lumber is natural colored, environmentally friendly, causes less corrosion of fasteners, and meets all code requirements.

The tops of our flight pens are covered with 1" knotted, Nylon, game bird netting. This type of netting was chosen for its durability, flexibility, and appearance. The 1" netting will prevent feral birds from entering the pens and will prevent peafowl from becoming entangled when they fly up into it. Knotted netting is smaller in diameter than knitted netting so it won't collect as much snow and become weighted down during the winter months. We purchased a 50' x 100' panel of netting for our pens so that there are no seams or splices.

The sides of our flight pens are covered with PVC-coated welded wire. This wire is corrosion resistant and will maintain its nice appearance for the life of the pens. PVC coated wire can be quite expensive. We were able to save about 40% off of the price of the wire by purchasing factory seconds. The wire quality and PVC coating are the same as factory firsts but there is normally a minor manufacturing defect in each roll that off grades the entire roll. Most of the time, the defect was so minor that we easily made a small patch or were able to plan around the defect and cut it out of the roll as we used the wire.

The perimeter sides of the pens are covered with 1" x 1" wire to prevent feral birds and small predators from being able to enter the pens. The interior pen sides are covered with 1" x 2" wire. Since the top and exterior sides are feral bird proof, money was saved by using the 1" x 2" wire on the interior sides. A pneumatic stapler was used to attach all of the wires to the pens. The galvanized staples were 1 ¼" in length and with a ½" crown. The staples were spaced about 8" to 10" apart. The perimeter of the pens is protected from digging predators by burying 1" x 2" wire underground. An electric fence wire is added mid-height of the pen sides to prevent any predators from climbing up the sides to try to chew through the top netting.

Many of the design ideas incorporated in our flight pens were gathered during visits to fellow peafowl breeders' farms, visits to zoos across the US, and livestock auctions attended. No matter where you go, ideas can be observed and documented for future use. A digital camera is an invaluable tool for documenting new ideas. Some of the best ideas that I have seen in person have been during the farm visit days of the annual UPA, Inc. conventions held each fall.

Pavo Muticus

(Green Peafowl)

by: Craig Hopkins

I am providing you with the following information so that you understand the special needs of the green peafowl that you are considering. Green peafowl is one of two "wild" colors of peafowl. The other one is the Pavo cristatus or better known as the India blue peafowl. Their care requirements are as different as their physical appearance.

There are three subspecies of green peafowl. They are Muticus-Muticus (Java), Muticus-Imperator (Indo-Chinese), and Muticus-Spicifer (Burmese). All of these subspecies have subtle differences in coloration and confirmation.

When you receive your green peafowl, put them in a small building, box stall, chicken house, or utility shed. It is a good idea to isolate the birds, if possible, for a couple of weeks to make sure that they are adjusted to their new environment before introducing them to other birds. Sometimes the birds that you already have will pick on new birds. You do not want your new birds to have to compete for food and water while they are settling into their new home. Green peafowl are prone to feather picking so do not overcrowd them. If several green peafowls are to be kept in a small area, anti-pick devices may have to be used. Green peafowl is more aggressive by nature so they may pick on your other peafowl if they are in a small area as well.

If the building or stall has glass windows, cover the windows with wire or Plexiglas so that the glass will not get broken by the birds flying into it. Green peafowl are much more excitable and nervous by nature than the common peafowl. I play a radio on low volume with these birds since they are hatched so they will be accustomed to strange noises. When entering their pen, talk to them or whistle softly as you enter the pen so that they know that you are entering their pen. Do not make sudden moves or loud noises while in the pen.

Make sure that the door or gate to their pen will close by itself behind you. They are strong flyers and can fly out an open door before you know it.

In areas where wintertime temperatures plunge well below freezing, additional heat should be provided to keep the building between 30- and 40-degrees F. A heated roost can also be used to keep their feet and legs from experiencing frostbite. The heated roost consists of an electric heat tape attached to a 2 x 4 and covered with short, pile carpeting.

Green peafowl of ages 6 months and older can be fed the same diet as the common peafowl breeds. Avoid high protein feeds such as turkey feeds. Peafowl is the largest member of the pheasant family and they should be fed game bird or pheasant diets rather than chicken or turkey diets. Green peachicks under 6 months of age should be fed a low-protein diet to prevent slipped leg tendons. I use a low protein, medicated, chicken starter for all of my peachicks.

As the green peafowl reach breeding age, the males can become very aggressive towards one another, the hens, and their owners. It is a good idea to have plenty of roosts in their pen and places for the peahens to hide from an aggressive male. I would not keep 2 breeding-age males together in the same pen during the breeding season. Protect yourself when entering a pen with a breeding-age male because many males show no fear of humans and will come and challenge you at the gate. Be very careful if a breeding-age male is roosting above your head. They like to fly down on top of you and attack.

If you need to catch your green peafowl for any reason, I recommend that you do it after dark. They are much easier to catch and handle when it is dark. They will not try to fly through windows or to the top of their pen once it is dark. Many green peafowls have been killed during handling because they flew through a window or flew up and broke their neck when they hit the ceiling. Use a strong fishing net to catch the birds. Never grab them by the wings or by just one leg. Catch them in the fishing net and grab both legs at the same time and hold the legs together above the knee joint. Allow the bird to kick its legs. Do not try to hold the legs just above the feet because the knee joint can be damaged or a leg can be broken.

Proper handling of green peafowl will prevent injuries to the birds and to you and it will lessen the chances that the birds will go into shock.

Green peafowl are one of the rarest and most beautiful peafowl available and well worth the extra work that it takes to raise them. They are the closest relative to a truly wild peacock and they take some special care to raise them. I hope that you enjoy your green peafowl.

BLENDING FEEDS AT HOME
IS JUST NOT A GOOD IDEA

by: Doug Buffington

If you ask 100 people what they are feeding their peacocks you will get 100 different responses. Many are blending different bagged feeds together, while adding scratch grains and other ingredients, with the intention of somehow improving the nutritional value. In reality, the nutritional value is compromised by this practice. The result is a hodge-podge of unknown nutrition where critical balances of phosphorus, calcium and vitamin D3 are upset. Protein levels are also disturbed.

Adding scratch and other grains to the diet of a balanced and complete feed will cause an imbalance of the "Cal-Phos" ratio. When phosphorus levels are too high and calcium too low, the phosphorus will pull the calcium it needs not only from eggshell production but also from the beak, bones, and other vital areas where calcium is required. Egg binding in hens is frequently attributed to the low calcium level of scratch grains as grains are high in phosphorous and low in calcium. Additionally, a lower level of vitamin D3 achieved by home blending will lower a peacock's ability to absorb calcium.

The level of protein is also left undetermined in home blended feeds. And, mixing medicated starters with other feeds will reduce the level of Amprolium, in medicated starters, below the therapeutic level necessary to control Coccidiosis. For the first three to four months, feed chicks a medicated starter with a protein level not greater than 20%. Protein levels above 20% will cause a crippling overgrowth of the legs and toes.

Older chicks and adults can be fed the Purina flock raiser and especially the Purina Game Bird Layer during the laying season. Feed these straight from the bag without blending them with anything else. Feed the Purina Flock Raiser in the off-season.

EGG BINDING

SYMPTOMS, PREVENTION AND TREATMENT

By: Doug Buffington

One of the most common laying issues is an egg-bound hen

CAUSES: An egg-bound hen has an egg that is lodged in the oviduct and cannot pass out of the body. Left untreated, egg binding is a potentially fatal condition. Hens that do not pass a bound egg within 24 hours will usually die. Hens can become egg-bound for a number of reasons. One cause of egg binding may be the result of a hen trying to pass an unusually large egg. Egg binding can also occur in hens that are laying their first eggs. Primarily, their system lacks sufficient calcium. To maintain the muscle strength necessary to lay an egg, a peahen must be fed a diet with 3% or more calcium. To prevent any thin or soft shells from showing up, feed the Purina Game Bird Layer with a 3% calcium content. Begin the Game Bird Layer one month before the first egg is expected. Both the eggs and the quality of the feathers will be improved with the Purina Flock Raiser and the Purina Game Bird Layer. When the laying season is over, resume feeding the Flock Raiser. Chicken layer pellets will have a 5% calcium level that some consider too high to be fed to peacocks all during the year. Many complain that a higher calcium level fed all during the year is not good for the kidneys. And, the lower protein level of chicken feed will not provide the best feather quality.

SYMPTOMS: If your hen is egg-bound, it will most likely exhibit symptoms that tell you there is an issue. These symptoms can include:

- Lethargy
- Straining
- Panting
- Paralysis
- Uncharacteristic sitting/squatting
- Tail pumping up and down
- Change in normal behavior
- Stilt-like walking characteristic of a penguin.

PREVENTION: Feed the Purina Game Bird Layer as the main ration during the laying season beginning one month before the first egg is expected. Treats should be no more than 10% of the total diet and they should never include mealworms. Peacocks will easily become addicted to them and begin to abandon their regular feed while they wait for more mealworms.

The Purina Flock Raiser is a good feed for peacocks after the laying season. Chicks can be converted to the Flock Raiser after 3 to 4 months of the medicated Purina Start & Grow. Move the Breeders to the Purina Game Bird Layer one month before the laying season then back to the Flock Raiser after the season. These feeds along with the medicated Purina Start and Grow can be found at Tractor Supply or at any Purina dealer.

Never feed scratch grains to your peacocks. They are the lowest cost but contain the lowest levels of nutritional value, especially calcium. Remember that things are cheap for a reason. Peacocks will not maintain the best health with scratch grains nor will their feathers be of the best quality and color. Because grains are high in phosphorus, and very low in calcium, the difference will be made up when the phosphorus begins to pull the calcium needed for laying eggs from the bones, beak and muscles. Depleting calcium from the muscles will contribute to egg binding.

The very best feed for peafowl, during the laying season, is the Purina Game Bird Layer. It will not need a calcium supplement like oyster shell. In the off season, feed the Purina Flock Raiser. Begin feeding the Purina Game Bird Layer to peacocks one month before the first egg is expected.

In the absence of the Purina Game Bird Layer during the laying season, feed the Purina Flock Raiser and provide oyster shell as free choice. Keep all of the feeds as a crumble to ease the transition from one to another during the year.

TREATMENT: A hen with a low calcium level can most often be unbound by giving one Tums tablet broken into 4 pieces. Open the beak and press each piece against the side and slide it down the throat past the trachea being careful not to get it into the trachea. A Tums tablet will have 1,000mgs of calcium. The calcium in a Tums tablet will add enough strength to the muscles for a hen to lay the bound egg within a few minutes to a few hours.

Beyond all else, do not break a bound egg internally. This will leave sharp edged egg shell that will possibly set up a peritonitis infection. If an egg is broken internally, immediately give a 3/4cc SubQ injection or a drench of Oxytetracycline that is most commonly sold as Duramycin 72-200 and LA 200. A 500mg tablet of Aqua-Mox can also be given.

ARE PUMPKIN SEEDS A DEWORMER

by: Dr. Ruediger Hauck

Auburn University, College of Veterinary Medicine

Every fall, posts begin to appear on Facebook and in blogs about using pumpkin seeds as a natural dewormer for chickens. But this popular claim begs the question as to whether or not the product actually works to control worms. Finally, research at the laboratory of Dr. Ruediger Hauck at Auburn University has answered this age-old question.

Most backyard flock owners have laying hens, so Dr Hauck's study focused on this type. Powdered pumpkin seed was used to treat worms in the Single Comb White Leghorn. The study also looked at another, much more commonly known plant that has a long history of use as a dewormer (or vermifuge): *Artemisia absinthium* is otherwise known as wormwood. Both ingredients were incorporated into the birds' evenly so the chickens could not pick out ingredients so we could be certain the birds were actually consuming the ingredient. The powered pumpkin seed was included in the feed at a rate of 1% and the powdered wormwood was included at a rate of 0.02%.

The laying hens were raised on a regular diet until they were 16 weeks old and then were placed in cages and the new diets were begun. One group was fed a control diet with no test ingredients.

When the chickens were 25 weeks old, half of the birds in each group were given a dose of 250 *Ascaridia galli* eggs. *Ascaridia galli* is a roundworm that affects the digestive tract of chickens and other poultry. Feces were collected regularly to see if the diets affected the amount of worm eggs in the droppings.

Additionally, adult worms were counted in the digestive tract to see if the diets affected their numbers. Chicken eggs were collected daily and tested to see if the treatments had any effect on the quality of the eggs. The study ended when the chickens were 35 weeks old.

The results... When it came down to counting the number of adult worms found in the digestive tract there was no statistical difference between any of the groups. The treatments of wormwood and pumpkin seed did not affect the number of adult worms in the gut.

PEACOCK MEDICATIONS IN THE UK & EU

By: Doug Buffington

Medications for animals and their distribution are more tightly regulated in the UK and the EU. The result is that all have been removed from the shelf and even medicated starter feed is not available. However, pigeon medications are still allowed to be sold without a Vet's script and can be ordered online.

HARKERS 4 IN 1

Coccidiosis, Blackhead (histomoniasis), Canker (trichomoniasis), Worms, Lice, Mites, Fleas and ticks can be treated in peacocks with the Harkers 4 in 1. Simply add 6ml to one liter (quart) of drinking water mixed up fresh daily for 5 to 7 days and kept out of the sun. Mix up only what is needed for one day's consumption. For the medicated water to be effective, it must be provided to sickly peacocks that are still eating and drinking normally. A sickly bird that has stopped eating and drinking can be treated by inserting one full eyedropper (1ml) of the Harkers 4 in 1, full strength, directly down the throat for 5 to 7 days or for as long as the symptoms persist. Be sure to insert the eye dropper or syringe off to the side of the trachea and not into it. If you are treating Blackhead and Coccidiosis, continue the treatment until there is no more yellow or red in the poop. For Canker, it is regrettable but the Harkers 4 in 1 is only a treatment and not generally a cure. A Canker treatment may take 2 to 4 weeks. Follow ups may be necessary. When treating for Coccidiosis, Canker and Blackhead, wash the drinking container daily with bleach water.

You may need to search a few sites but the Harkers 4 in 1 is available with a payment in Euros, Pounds and the American dollar. It may also be available on Amazon in some countries.

Dac FMT Powder

Dac FMT is a powder that can be added to drinking water at the rate of 2 teaspoons per gallon of drinking water. Only mix up what is needed for one day's consumption, provide it fresh daily and keep it out of the sun. The medicated water should be the only drinking source available to a sick bird for 5 to 7 days. But maintain the treatment as long as the symptoms persist. It will treat Coccidiosis, Blackhead (histomoniasis), Heximita and Canker (trichomoniasis) only. It will not treat worms, lice, mites and ticks. A medication for worms should be given with the Dac FMT treatment. If your bird is not eating or drinking, use the Harkers liquid 4 in 1 as described above. If you are treating Blackhead, continue the treatment until there is no more yellow in the poop. For Canker, it is regrettable but the Harkers 4 in 1 is only a treatment and not generally a cure You will need to search a few sites but both medications are available with a payment in Euros, Pounds and the American dollar. The Dac FMT powder and Harkers 4 in 1 may be available on Amazon in some countries.

When treating for Coccidiosis, Canker and Blackhead, wash the drinking container daily with bleach water.

WHAT TO FEED A PEACOCK

By: Doug Buffington

The nutritionist, Dr. Biggs PhD at Purina, recommends feeding the Purina Flock Raiser when the birds are out of season. It is 20% protein with 1% calcium. Then, a month before the first eggs are expected, he advises to put the peacocks on the Purina Game Bird Layer with 18% protein with 3% calcium. The Purina Game Bird Layer is reported to be optimally formulated for egg production, egg shell quality and hatchability along with improved chick vigor. One additional benefit is that both feeds are a crumble. This makes it easier to transition chicks after 3 to 4 months of the medicated Purina Start & Grow crumble to the Flock Raiser crumble with 20% protein and 1% calcium then on to the Purina Game Bird Layer crumble. Return to the Purina Flock Raiser after the laying season.

The Flock Raiser and Game Bird Layer can be sourced from any Purina dealer or at Tractor Supply.

Many are advocates of free ranging for the natural variety it adds to a bird's diet. But free ranging is not the wonderful experience that it is made out to be. Free ranged peacocks are unlikely to pick up anything with more than 8 to 10% protein and who knows about the necessary vitamins, minerals and amino acids. Many also think highly about the protein value of the insets that peacocks will find free ranging. But in reality, how many bugs will be available in the fall and during the winter? Additionally, insects and earth worms are often intermediate host for Blackhead and other diseases. Purina does not advise that more than 10% of a farm bird's diet be something other than the bagged feed so as not to upset the balances of calcium, phosphorous, proteins, amino acids, vitamins and other necessary ingredients. Scratch grains are the worst to mix in with any other type of poultry feed because it is so nutritionally poor.

Here is the takeaway… feed your chicks the medicated Purina Start & Grow for a minimum of 3 to 4 months. Then go to the Purina Flock Raiser crumble. For breeder birds, begin feeding the Purina Game Bird Layer crumble one month before the first eggs are expected. After the breeding season, return to the Flock Raiser crumble. Feeding crumbles makes it easier to transition your peacocks from one feed to another. This is especially important for young birds that will have a difficult time with pellets.

DENTAL SYRINGES FOR SYRINGING MEDICATIONS

By: Doug Buffington

Dental syringes are perfect for oral dosing medications. If you are not comfortable with giving an injection, you can drench antibiotics and the Ivermectin 1%, Safeguard and Moxivet Plus. Be sure to insert the syringe tip down the throat off to the side of the trachea and not into it. The Syringes are also good for drenching 5 cc's/mls water medicated with the All in One, Metronidazole and Ronidazole 20% to sick birds that are no longer eating or drinking. Dissolve two, 250mg Metronidazole tablets into 5cc's of water, draw it up and insert the tip into the throat off to the side of the trachea and inject it. A 250mg Metronidazole tablet is often difficult, for those without experience, to get down the throat without getting it into the trachea. Give two, 250mg metronidazole powder packs to 5cc's of water if you cannot find tablets. The tablets and powders are often sold by pigeon supply and fish antibiotic sites as Fish Zole, Fix Zole and the API General Cure. Sometimes a Vet may let you have them without bringing a sick bird to the office. The syringe prices will vary so scroll through Amazon pages for the best price. Search for "straight tip dental syringes." You can also use curved tip syringes found at pharmacies and on Amazon if the straight tipped is not available. The syringes can be washed out and reused. If necessary, a bit of the tip can be removed to help draw up the solution.

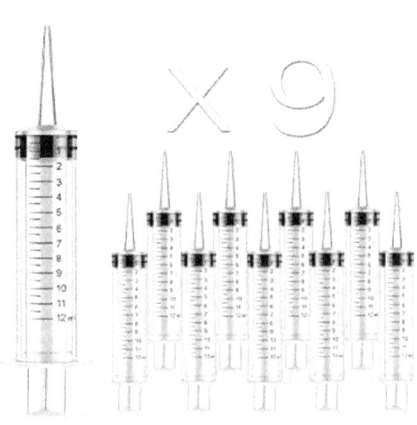

WHAT TO REMEMBER ABOUT BLACKHEAD, COCCIDIOSIS AND CANKER

By: Doug Buffington

If a peacock is breathing normally but walking around with droopy wings or is sitting on the pen floor lethargic and looking sleepy eyed it likely has the beginning stages of Blackhead or Coccidiosis. In more acute cases, Blackhead symptoms will include a yellow discharge in the poop. The yellow is liver bile that is discharged when a peacock's liver is being attacked by the histomona protozoan that is a parasite on the cecal worm. Coccidiosis will show as blood in the poop in acute cases.

The Canker symptom will show as a whitish to yellowish growth in the beak, on the tongue and in the throat. Left untreated, the growth will continue until a peacock can no longer eat, drink or even breath. It must be remembered that medications for Canker are only treatments and generally not a cure. Follow up treatments are often necessary. Segregate any infected peacocks. Canker is commonly spread by pigeons and doves that eat and drink with peacocks and other farm birds.

Relieving the worm burden of a peacock with a worm medication is an important part of the Blackhead treatment as the cecal worm is the host for the Blackhead protozoan. A grown peacock should also receive two 250mg tablets of metronidazole daily for 5 to 7 days or for as long as the red or yellow discharge in the poop persist. Ronidazole 20% powder is an effective Blackhead and Canker treatment if an infected bird is drinking normally.

When a peacock is still eating and drinking normally it can be treated with the All in One for 5 to 7 days or as long as there is red or yellow in the poop. Supplement this treatment with metronidazole tablets. A sick peacock that is eating can additionally be fed scrambled eggs lightly dusted with the All-in-One powder to increase its intake of the medication. The active ingredients of the All in One will treat Coccidiosis, Canker and Blackhead as well as worms.

Complete the deworming by following the end of the All-in-One treatment, ten days after the end of the first treatment, with another round of the All in One. This will catch the worms that have hatched from eggs left behind during the first worming from the All in One.

Canker can be treated with two, 250mg metronidazole tablets given daily for 10 days to 2 weeks. Follow up treatments will likely be necessary. A number of powdered medications for the drinking water are also available to treat Canker. Make sure that your peacock is drinking normally enough to take up a therapeutic dose. A favored powdered medication to treat Canker and Blackhead is the Ronidazole 20% available at pigeon supply sites. Check and segregate all infected birds. When treating Canker and other protozoan infections, wash out all drinking containers with bleach water daily. Keep medicated water out of the sun.

HOW AMPROLIUM WORKS

by: Doug Buffington

Many have the misguided notion that starter feeds, medicated with Amprolium, are somehow unhealthy for chicks. Some will even say that it is a vitamin B blocker that kills chicks. The following will explain how Amprolium works to control Coccidiosis and to build chick resistance.

Amprolium is a common anticoccidial medication used for the prevention of coccidiosis in young chickens, turkeys, peafowl, guinea and game birds. **The thiamine transport system in the coccidiosis parasite is more sensitive to Amprolium than that of the host. More of the Amprolium will enter the coccidian protozoan to limit its absorption of vitamin B1.** Amprolium works by mimicking thiamine (vitamin B1) that coccidia need to develop and reproduce. When the coccidia ingest Amprolium, it will experience a thiamin deficiency and starve from malnutrition. Medicated starters are dosed to allow a small amount of the Coccidia to survive that stimulate the immune system to build a resistance to it. Vitamin B1 is not completely shut off. Additionally, Amprolium will not affect the levels of B12, B6 or B3. In the United States, it is one of the few medications approved by the FDA for use with egg laying chicken hens. There is no required egg withdrawal.

Blending a medicated starter with other feeds will reduce the Amprolium ingredient below a therapeutic level necessary to control Coccidiosis. Medicated starters need to constitute a 90% minimum of a chick's diet to effectively control the Coccidia protozoan. Building an immune resistance to Coccidiosis will require a minimum of 3 to 4 months after hatching. However, it is not harmful to feed medicated starters to young birds beyond 3 to 4 months. It will only affect the Coccidia protozoa that may be present. Hens that remain with chicks may also consume the stater feed.

However, medicated starters are not recommended for ducks, geese and other waterfowl as medicated feeds lack the level of vitamin B3 (niacin) necessary for good health and development. Waterfowl will need an unmedicated starter with a more fortified level of niacin. During their developmental period of growth, waterfowl will need 2 to 3 times more niacin than other farm birds until they are full grown at 18 to 20 weeks old.

GAPEWORMS

by: Tim Daniels

Gapeworms *(Syngamus*

Gapeworms, more common in pheasants and partridges, are included under the category of the "respiratory system" since the adult worms reside in the trachea (or windpipe) and often produce a gurgling or 'tracheal rattle' that can be confused with respiratory problems. It also affects chickens, guinea fowl, peafowl, game birds and turkeys. Gasping for breath or "gaping", as it is known, is the most common symptom of gapeworm. Shaking of the head and neck stretching are also common. When birds are held, gurgling can often be heard which is a "tracheal rattle." Gasping for breath caused by gapeworms is often confused with respiratory problems. If a heavy infestation occurs, death by suffocation will result.

Gapeworm infestation can occur either directly, by birds eating eggs that have been swallowed or coughed up by infested birds, or indirectly by intermediate hosts such as earthworms or snails. Once gapeworms are present in a flock there must be an ongoing treatment. However, most worm products will treat for it.

But gapeworm is incredibly hardy, and will remain viable in the soil for more than four years, infecting and reinfecting a flock. The good news is that gapeworms are not common among backyard flocks.

Young birds up to 8 weeks of age are particularly susceptible to gapeworm. Gapeworms normally live in the trachea (windpipe) but are also found in the bronchi and lungs.

When gapeworm eggs hatch, the larvae penetrate the intestine walls and move to the lungs and bronchi. It is here that they go through a larval molt, before travelling up to the trachea by way of the lungs. Male and female gapeworms attach to one another once they arrive there. This process takes around 7 days. Fully grown, they are "Y" shaped and vary in size from 1 to 2cm long and red in color.

Other Names: Gapes, Red worms, Forked worms.

Symptoms: Gasping (gaping), yawning, gurgling/respiratory distress, head shaking, loss of appetite, and eventually coughing and choking.

Area affected: Trachea (windpipe), bronchi and lungs.

Transmission: Via intermediate hosts such as earthworms, snails, insects and directly by poultry picking up eggs that have been coughed up, or passed out into feces.

Prevention: A good worming strategy.

Treatment: Favored treatments are Levamisole (Prohibit), Moxivet Plus, Safeguard, Ivermectin 1% and Ivermectin Pour-On. Look for Flubenvet in the UK and EU.

WHAT CANKER LOOKS LIKE IN PEACOCKS

by: Doug Buffington

The photo below is one example of what pigeon canker looks like in peacocks. Left untreated it will continue to grow until your peacock can no longer eat, drink or even breath. It can be treated with two 250mg tablets of metronidazole daily as a single dose for 10 days to 2 weeks. If an infected peacock is drinking normally, the water can also be treated with Ronidazole 20% sourced from Pigeon Supplies Plus and other pigeon supply sites. It is regrettable that these treatments are generally not a cure. Follow up treatments will likely be necessary.

Canker is spread by pigeons and doves that feed and drink with your peacocks. Segregate all infected birds. When treating infected peacocks, wash out all drinking containers daily with bleach water.

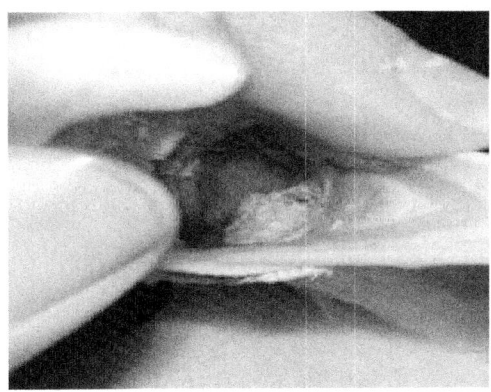

MEDICATIONS TO KEEP ON HAND

Durvet Duramycin 72-200 (LA 200)

Found at feed stores with Vet's Script

Prohibit (Levamisole)

Commonly found on the internet and Ebay

Metronidazole tablets (250mgs)

Found at pigeon supply and fish antibiotic

sites without a Vet's Script

Aqua Mox & Doxy Mox tablets

Commonly found without a Vet's Script

at pigeon supply and fish antibiotic sites

ALL in ONE

Found at Pigeon Supplies Plus and other pigeon supply sites

Ronidazole 20%

Found at Pigeon Supplies Plus and other pigeon supply sites

Moxivet Plus

Found at Pigeon Supplies Plus and other pigeon supply sites

Worm Medications

(In the EU and UK…Search the internet for the Harker's 4 in 1

EU and UK MEDICATIONS Search the internet for the Harker's 4 in 1 and the Dac FMT (All Around Mix) to treat Coccidiosis, Blackhead, and Canker. Also look for the Flubenvet, Fenbendazole and Ivermectin wormers.

The medications listed above can be used to treat any farm bird. Although Moxivet, Ronidazole, Dimetridazole and Metronidazole tablets are not recommended for animals that will become a part of the food supply. An egg withdrawal has yet to be established.

At a minimum, stock a worm medication, an antibiotic, the All in One and metronidazole tablets.

TRICHOMONIASIS
(PIGEON CANKER)

By: Douglas Buffington

Trichomonas gallinae is a protozoan parasite that can infect every kind of bird from a canary to an ostrich. It is an ancient pathogen that is reported to find its origins in therapod dinosaurs although one would wonder how. It is pandemic among pigeons today. Eighty percent of them will carry it. Trichomonas is generally found in the oral-nasal cavity or in the anterior end of the digestive and respiratory tracts. This translates into the upper inside of the beak, on the tongue and around the trachea. Peafowl and other farm birds can become infected through food and drinking water contaminated with feces, saliva and crop secretions. Doves and pigeons that eat and drink with peacocks or other farm birds will spread Trichomonas to them. Even wild birds can spread this infection more commonly known as pigeon canker.

Early lesions that first appear as small white to yellowish areas in the mouth cavity will consist of inflammation and ulceration of the mucosal surface. The lesions increase in size and number and extend to the esophagus and crop. The lesions may develop into large, firm necrotic masses that eventually block the throat and trachea. Left untreated your peacocks and other infected farm birds will eventually be unable to eat, drink or even breathe.

One of the first symptoms to be observed is a peacock that exhibits a repeated gapping or opening and closing of the beak as it struggles to breathe. This same symptom is also characteristic of a respiratory infection. An open beak examination should be performed every time a peacock is gapping with labored breathing to determine the cause.

Trichomonas is often treated with metronidazole tablets, All in One, Ronidazole 20% and other powders to medicate the drinking water. Look for them at pigeon supply sites. It must be emphasized that these medications are treatments, but regrettably, they are generally not a cure. Follow up treatments will likely be necessary. Veterinarians, suppliers of pigeon medications and even professors at colleges of Veterinary Science cannot offer a cure. When treating for canker, segregate infected farm birds. Infected peacocks should never be allowed to free range or otherwise have contact with uninfected peacocks. They should be permanently segregated from the flock. When purchasing peacocks, it is imperative to open the beak and examine for canker. Peacocks with the white to yellow growths must be rejected. It may be properly assumed that others in the flock are also infected.

CANKER TREATMENT

(TRICHOMONIASIS)

Department of Natural Resources

Trichomoniasis is caused by *Trichomonas gallinae*, a single-celled, pear-shaped protozoan with 4 whip-like anterior flagella and a fin-like undulating membrane that extends for approximately 2/3 of the total body length. The protozoan moves by undulation and flagellar action. Trichomoniasis is also known as Canker. The severity of the disease to the bird depends on the susceptibility of the bird and the pathogenic potential of the strain of the parasite.

Distribution

Trichomoniasis is cosmopolitan in distribution. In captive birds, the disease has been found in domestic pigeons, doves, quail, turkeys, peafowl, chickens, falcons, hawks, various finches, the Java sparrow, and canaries. In wild birds, the disease has been found in doves and feral pigeons throughout the U.S. In Michigan, mourning doves and feral pigeons have been positive for trichomoniasis. The disease is believed to have been first introduced to North America when infected doves were brought from France to Nova Scotia in the early 1600's. Trichomoniasis is the most important disease of Mourning Doves in North America.

Transmission

Transmission of *T. gallinae* occurs by discharge of bodily fluids in one of four ways. Adult doves and pigeons infect their offspring during feeding, infect other adult birds through contaminated food, water, and bedding and via courtship behavior. Raptors are infected through consumption of infected doves or pigeons.

This is a disease primarily of doves and pigeons and is transmitted from the adult to their offspring by the regurgitation method of feeding used by these birds. *T. gallinae* is present in the back of the throat of carrier birds (carrier birds may carry the infection for a year or longer). The trichomonads can easily mix with food and the pigeon milk that is produced in the crop of the bird and be transmitted when the parent bird regurgitates this mixture to its offspring. Oftentimes the offspring is infected at its first feeding which can occur minutes after hatching. This infection may become asymptomatic or may progress to a fatal case in 4 to 18 days post-infection.

Transmission via contamination of food and water occurs when the bird has extensive oral lesions and is unable to swallow food material or water. This results in pieces of grain or water being placed in the mouth, contaminated by organisms, and then dropped back on the ground, in the feeder, or in the water source. When another bird feeds or drinks in this location, *T. gallinae* is ingested and an infection may result. This organism can live at least 5 days on some moist grains and 20 minutes to several hours in water.

The organism is extremely sensitive to desiccation (drying) as there is no cyst or resistant stage of the life cycle. Bedding is infected with the organism via fecal contamination.

During courtship, doves and pigeons have direct bill to bill contact during cross feeding and billing (touching of bills).

Birds of prey contract an infection by consuming infected doves or pigeons.

Clinical signs

Birds infected with *T. gallinae* display a variety of clinical signs. The birds are depressed, salivate excessively, are emaciated, appear listless, ruffled and dull, have difficulty closing their mouth, display repeated swallowing movements, exhibit open mouth and noisy breathing, watery eyes, difficulty eating and drinking, difficulty standing or maintaining their balance, have diarrhea, may have a puffy appearance of the neck, exhibit a sunken and empty crop and have a fetid odor. Birds will usually die from starvation due to the blockage of the esophagus or from suffocation caused by blockage of the trachea by the caseous, cheese-like, necrotic masses in the mouth commonly seen with this disease.

Pathology

The pathology associated with trichomoniasis in doves and pigeons usually involves young birds and consists of the formation of caseous necrotic masses in the upper digestive tract and occasionally in the viscera. The first acute lesions appear in the mouth, pharynx, esophagus, and crop. They will consist of inflammation and the development of creamy-white, wet, and sticky exudate on the mucosal surface lining. The lesions progress to small, well-defined raised yellow-white ulcers. As the disease progresses the mucosal lesions become yellow in color, larger in size, hard, caseous coalesced masses that may invade the sinuses of the skull, extend externally to the beak and eyes, penetrate through the base of the skull into the brain and penetrate the viscera causing necrotic areas in the liver, spleen, pancreas, heart, lungs and air sacs. In raptors, liver and abdominal lesions are the main pathological changes that occur.

Diagnosis

Diagnosis of trichomoniasis is based on history, clinical signs, lesions, and identification of the organism microscopically and by culturing. Gross lesions consist of yellow-white caseous necrotic obstructive nodules in the oral cavity, esophagus and crop. Under low power magnification, the trichomonad organism can be found in the saliva or in smears of the cheese-like necrotic lesions in the upper digestive tract. These samples must be collected within 48 hours of the bird's death to be viable.

Treatment

Treatment is only feasible in captive birds because the drugs used for treatment must be administered orally, either by force feeding or by treating the food and/or water. Antiprotozoal medications that have been used are two, 250mg Metronidazole tablets daily for 10 days to 2 weeks and Ronidazole 20% powder for the drinking water if an infected bird is drinking well enough to take up a therapeutic dose for two to four weeks.

Control

In order to control trichomoniasis, sources of infection need to be eliminated. In captive birds, regularly disinfect food and water sources with 10% bleach solution. Keep medicated water out of the sun. Screen out wild birds to protect from contamination by wild pigeons and other birds.

DOUG'S NOTE: It is regrettable but Canker medications should be regarded as treatments that are generally not a cure. Follow up treatments will likely be necessary. Infected birds should remain segregated and not allowed to free range with other farm birds. **When treating for Coccidiosis, Canker and Blackhead, wash the drinking container daily with bleach water. Make up medicated drinking water fresh daily and keep it out of the sun.**

DO NOT BRING PEACOCKS HOME FROM THE AUCTION

by: Douglas Buffington

I am sure that many who sell peafowl are offering healthy birds at the auction but watch for those who are not. Be especially cautious of breeders who are bringing in 25 to 50 birds. This may mean that their pens have been recently culled.

For too many peacocks, the auction will be the last stop for birds that are too old, crippled, blind and infected with who knows what. Resist the urge to rescue them. It is like going to the leper colony to adopt a child.

Do not bring a peacock home from anywhere without looking into its open beak and down the throat for pigeon canker (trichomoniasis). Also notice if it has infected eyes, or a limp. Quarantine new additions to a flock for a month and give a seven day treatment of the All in One medication followed up with another round ten days after the end of the first treatment. This will deworm the peacock plus combat Blackhead, Coccidiosis and pigeon Canker. Watch for red or yellow in the poop as it is a symptom of acute Coccidiosis and Blackhead (histomoniasis). Before buying, pick up the peacock and feel its keel to see if it is emaciated and underweight. This inspection will signal that a bird is malnourished or likely sick with something. When treating for Coccidiosis, Canker and Blackhead, wash the drinking container with bleach water and mix up the medicated water fresh daily. Keep it out of the sun.

CLOSING REMARKS

You are at the end of your study in peacock care. It has been the intention of this publication to make breeders more successful with their birds and to lift the standard of care for peacocks.

The peacock is an ancient bird that has captured the affection of people throughout time. It is sometimes said that peacocks should come with a warning label because they are so addictive. With the exception of the polar caps, there is no place in this world where peacocks are not kept. It is a tropical bird that has adapted itself to climates from Scandinavia to the bottom of Africa. Peacocks are top to bottom in South America too. We hope that many of you will join our Peacocks Only group on Facebook. It is a place where we share information about all aspects of keeping peacocks and especially how to care for them should they become ill. It is our common purpose, as a community, to lift their standard of care and to share our love for them.

We hope you will join our Peacocks Only Facebook group. The popularity of the group has given rise to a number of similarly named groups. So, please be sure to choose the group simply named: Peacocks Only.

NOTES

Printed in Great Britain
by Amazon